Limit & Lead
Student Workbook

Matthew L. Ferrara, Ph.D.
Clinical and Forensic Psychology
2500 West William Cannon Drive Suite 703 Austin, TX 78745
Tele: 512-708-0502 Fax: 512-708-0557
mferraraphd@att.net

Limit and Lead Student Workbook
Version 5.00

Cover Image: The Phoenix is a colorful, mythical bird made of fire. Legend has it that the Phoenix can live as long as 1,000 years and at the end of its life, it builds a nest, settles into the nest and sets it ablaze. The Phoenix rises from the ashes of the nest and it is stronger than it was in its previous life. The Phoenix is a symbol of rebirth, change, and renewal. It is such a popular myth that many ancient civilizations adopted the Phoenix myth including Rome, Greece, Egypt, China and Phoenicia.

Table of Contents

MODULE THREE: SELF-CONTROL

MODULE FOUR: YOUR SUPPORT GROUP

MODULE FIVE: PREPARING FOR A CITIZEN LIFESTYLE

APPENDIX

Dear Fellow Traveler,

I know that you are on a journey. I might not have been down the path you are going down, but I have traveled far and wide. I know something about travel and travelers.

The first thing that you must know is that to travel and to be a traveler are not the same thing — just as a person and the path are different. A traveler chooses the travel. The person chooses the path. The key is choice.

Even though the key is choice, you must understand that you are not your choices. You make decisions but you are not your decisions. You choose a path but you are not the path. You are much more than that. A person is the sum of his or her experiences, intuitions, values, emotions, and knowledge as expressed in actions. We are in charge of our choices. We are not our choices.

If you chose badly in the past, that does not make you bad. If you chose badly in the past, your choice was bad. It is possible that the path you took was bad — but none of this can make you bad. Just as the person is not the path, a bad path does not make a person bad.

Bad choices can make for a bad journey. In your life, you will come to only a few major crossroads. The choices that you make at these crossroads will shape your life: make bad choices and you will have a bad life; make good choices and you will have a good life.

If you have made bad choices in the past, you probably don't like your life right now. There is good news for you, my fellow traveler: you can change your path. You can make different choices. You can change.

A journey requires change. Each step brings a new perspective. Each step brings change. Do not be afraid of the change — embrace it.

You can't stop change. Even if you try to keep your feet planted on the path and you try to not take a single step, the path will change on its own — as will everything around it. You are going to experience change no matter what, so you might as well choose the change you want. Choose wisely, though — especially if you are at a crossroads.

Never forget, my fellow traveler, that you are not the travel — you choose the travel. You are not your choices — you make your choices. Travel is change, and change cannot be avoided. Make good choices and you will have a good life. Make bad choices — well, you can always change.

Sincerely,

A fellow traveler

Assignment Tracking Form

Module One: Orientation and Getting Ready to Change

Date	Staff Initial	Goal – To prepare for treatment by gaining basic knowledge.
		1. Thinking Errors
		2. Thought Journal
		3. Criminal Outlets
		4. Criminal vs. Citizen Behavior
		5. Honesty
		6. How to Change
		7. Why Should I Change?
		8. Thinking Leads to Emotions and Behavior
		9. The Why Sandwich
		10. ACE: Self-Control Techniques
		11. My Role As a Member of My Treatment Team
		12. Module Test

Module Two: Honesty about Your Behaviors

Date	Staff Initial	Goal – To reveal everything about your offense and history. To show you have been honest by passing a polygraph about your offense.
		1. My Thoughts before My Instant Offense

		2. The Way I Felt about My Instant Offense
		3. My Fantasies about the Victim
		4. My Double Life
		5. GROUP ASSIGNMENT: OFFENSE SUMMARY WORKSHEET
		6. What I Learned about Myself from My Offense Summary Worksheet
		7. Criminal History Questionnaire
		8. GROUP ASSIGNEMNT: WHAT I LEARNED ABOUT MYSELF FROM MY CRIMINAL HISTORY

Module Three: Self-Control

Date	Staff Initial	Goal – To develop skills to control your criminal behavior and desires and to ensure that you have No More Victims.
		1. What are the Stair Steps?
		2. Coping with Triggers
		3. Coping with Thinking Errors
		4. Coping with Emotions
		5. Coping with Urges
		6. Coping with Set-Ups
		7. GROUP ASSIGNMENT: MY PLAN FOR GETTING OFF THE STAIR STEPS

Module Four: Create Your Support Group

Date	Staff Initial	Goal – To identify those individuals who will help you not return to using criminal behavior.
		1. I Need the Help of Those Who Love Me
		2. The People in My Support Group
		3. Letter to My Support Group
		4. **GROUP ASSIGMENT: CONTRACT WITH MY SUPPORT GROUP**
		5. Watch Out for Splitting
		6. Support Group Problem Solving

Module Five: Preparing for a Citizen Lifestyle

Date	Staff Initial	Goal – To complete assignments that will help you hold onto the positive changes you made during treatment.
		1. What Are My Old Habits?
		2. **GROUP ASSIGMENT: HABIT CONTROL**
		3. Making Change Last
		4. My High-Risk Situations
		5. Coping with Relapse
		6. **GROUP ASSIGNMENT: DISCHARGE SUMMARY**

Introduction

A lot of individuals have a fast-food approach to life, which leads them to say: *"I want what I want. I want it right now, and if you don't give it to me, I'll take it."* Do you know anybody who thinks like that? Do you think like that?

The fast-food approach to life sounds like a pretty good way to get what you want…or is it? Let's take a look at a few basics to see if the fast-food approach to life is really all that it's cracked up to be.

You're Outnumbered – You can count the number of adults in the United States who use a fast-food approach to life. They are in prison. At the end of 2012, there were about 1,570,000 men and women in prisons in the United States. At the same time, there were about 312,800,000 Americans not in prison. The good guys outnumbered the bad guys 312 to 1. Is that a big difference? Let's see: Imagine that a fight is about to happen. There are 312 guys on one side and one guy on the other side. Which side do you want to be on? No cheating – you can't say you would nuke the 312 good guys. If you answered the question honestly, you would say that you want to be on the side with 312 guys, and you don't want to be the lone guy about to get destroyed. If you use the fast-food approach to life, you are outnumbered. Eventually, the good guys will catch up to you and you will lose the fight.

You're Going to Get Caught – Let's stick with the idea that there are 312 good guys for every 1 bad guy in the United States. Imagine that the one bad guy is really, really, really smart. He's so smart that he has come up with the perfect crime, or so he thinks. He commits the "perfect" crime. How perfect does the perfect crime have to be? It has to be perfect enough that it can trick 312 good guys. The first good guy who investigates the perfect crime might not solve the crime. The second and third guy might not solve the crime, either, but maybe the 133rd good guy who investigates the crime uses some new crime-fighting technology. This good guy puts his head together with some of the other good guys who looked at the crime and…bingo! The crime is solved. The really, really, really smart bad guy is caught and he is put behind bars for a really, really, really long time.

It's Not a Good Way to Make Money – Some people who use the fast-food approach to life think that this approach is a good way to make money. It is not. There are many examples that can be used, but let's take a look at dealing drugs. The drug dealer says, *"I'm not about to get up at seven in the morning and go to work and work for eight hours and only get paid 80 dollars. I can make 1,000 dollars a day selling drugs."* He is right. One thousand dollars a day is a lot more money than 80 dollars a day…if the only day you look at is the day the drugs are sold. Let's say the drug dealer makes 1,000 dollars one day and he is arrested the next day. When he goes to court, he is sentenced to one year in jail. Drug dealers routinely get more than a year, but for the purpose of this example, we'll stick with one year as the amount of time the drug dealer spends in prison. To know how much the drug dealer makes per day, divide 1,000 dollars by the 365 days he spends in prison – the answer is $2.74. The drug dealer actually makes $2.74 per day, while the citizen makes $80.00 per day. If you look at annual income, the bad guy makes $1,000.00 per year and the good guy makes $13,000.00 per year. The fast-food approach to life is NOT a good way to make money.

You Don't Get to Keep What is Not Yours – Have you heard about what happens to the things bad guys "own" when they are arrested? When bad guys get arrested, the law takes their houses, cars, jewelry, clothes, and toys and sells them. Anything a bad guy gets by using the fast-food approach to life can be taken from him or her. How about the citizen who works for what he or she owns? If a bad guy takes a good guy's car, jewelry, toys or other belongings, the good guy can have his belongings returned by law enforcement. Citizens get to keep their belongings because they earned them – not so for bad guys.

The Fast Food Approach means Less Freedom – The bad guy who uses the fast-food approach to life often claims that it gives him more freedom, saying, *"I don't have to go to work or school. I don't have to wake up at any particular time. I stay out late."* All of those things are true. This is also true: when the bad guy meets his needs using the fast-food approach, the law says the bad guy is out of control, so they step in and control him. Once the bad guy is under the control of the law, he has a lot less freedom. So if you think short-term "freedom" is worth being on probation – or in prison, go ahead and make that deal. A smart person wouldn't.

You can believe what you want to believe about being a bad guy or about the fast-food approach to life, but the numbers don't lie. If you're a bad guy, you will get caught. Even if you're a really, really, really smart bad guy, you'll get caught and you will pay. While you are paying, you are losing time, freedom, money, and belongings. During this time, citizens are making more money, have more freedom, spend their time the way they want to, and are getting more belongings. Believe what you want, but a smart guy will do the math…and want to be a good guy.

The Purpose of this Workbook

If you are using the Limit & Lead Student Workbook, it means that you have used the fast-food approach to life and, consequently, your behavior has hurt someone. The goal of this workbook is to help you make a conversion from "old me" to "new me." If you do this, you'll be happy and successful, and you'll have **No More Victims**!

It is really important to understand that if you are a citizen, you can still satisfy all your needs and many of your wants. When you make the conversion to being citizen, the way you meet your needs changes.

- **Old Me** – When you use the fast food approach to life, you meet your needs in such a way that others are hurt and can't meet their own needs.
- **New Me** – As a citizen, you meet your needs in such a way that others can still meet their own needs.

It is not okay to hurt others just so you can have what you want. Every time you do that, you create a new victim. If you meet your needs the way citizens meet their needs, you can live a good life, a happy and successful life with **No More Victims!**

Structure of This Workbook

This workbook is divided into modules. A module is a collection of therapeutic homework assignments that deal with a particular therapeutic issue.

- **Orientation** – This module covers basic information used in treatment. You will learn important ideas, vocabulary, and self-control techniques.

- **Honesty about Your Criminal Behavior** – This module focuses on the way your behavior has hurt others. You take a close look at the behavior that got you put into this treatment program. You also take a look at your history of acting out. The goal of being honest about your behavior is twofold. First, you need to be honest and get things off your chest. Second, you need to be able to see your personal pattern of misconduct.

- **Self-Control** – This module helps you develop self-control. When you met your needs by creating victims, you were out of control, which is why others stepped in to control you. Would you like more freedom and independence? If so, learn self-control. If you use self-control, no one else has an excuse to come in and control you.

- **Your Support Group** – This module helps you get support from people in your life who are citizens.

- **Preparing for a Citizen Lifestyle** – By the time you start working on the assignments in this module, you have probably made some major changes in your life. The assignments in this module help you hold onto the positive changes you've made.

The assignments in these modules have been carefully developed to help you become happy and successful by using citizen behavior. If you follow the guidelines and principles in this workbook and become happy and successful, you will automatically reach the goal of this treatment program: **No More Victims!**

Assignments

In this program, you complete assignments from this workbook on your own time, not during therapy time. Think of the assignments as homework that you complete on your own. Whether you attend an individual therapy session or a group therapy session, bring a completed assignment with you.

The assignments in this workbook build upon each other. The assignments you complete in one module help you complete assignments in the next module. For example, the assignments in the Orientation Module will help you complete the assignments in the Honesty about Your Criminal Behavior Module.

Also, the assignments within a module build upon each other. Specifically, the assignments leading up to a group assignment help you complete the group assignment. There are very few assignments you actually present during a group therapy session, so most of your assignments will be reviewed when you meet one-on-one with your treatment provider.

Using Group Feedback

When you present an assignment in a group session, you will usually get a lot of feedback. Members of the group and your treatment provider will point out things you did not see. When you get feedback, your job is to write down the feedback. After the group session, you use the feedback to revise your assignment. You will then present the assignment again in a later group session. You will keep presenting an assignment again and again until your group members and treatment provider approve it.

Don't worry if you get a lot of feedback. Everybody has blind spots. Blind spots are areas where you cannot see yourself as you really are. It is embarrassing but true: even if we can't see into our own blind spots, other people can.

	Aware	**Unaware**
Self	Self-Awareness	Blind Spot
Others	Public Self	Private Self

Even though it may be embarrassing to have other people point out things you are not aware of, it is helpful. In therapy, when someone points out one of your blind spots, you can see yourself better. Your blind spot becomes smaller as you increase your self-awareness.

Proving that You Have Changed

The things that you learn by completing assignments in this workbook must make a difference in the way you behave. Put another way, what you learn during a treatment session must make a difference in the way that you behave outside of treatment sessions.

This program is not about completing assignments. This program is about changing the way that you think, feel, and behave, so that you have **No More Victims**! In this program, there are three ways that you can prove you have changed.

First, you can show that you have changed by how you behave during group therapy sessions. There are two things you can do during a group therapy session: give help and receive help. You give help when you give feedback to the other group members working on assignments. You receive help when you willingly accept the feedback you are given.

Second, you can show you have changed by the way that those who are close to you talk about you. The people who know you should be able to say that you have changed. You can expect that your treatment provider will to be talking to your loved ones to determine if you have changed.

Third, the staff persons who work with you should be able to see you've changed. If you are in a residential setting, like a halfway house, detention center, or training school, all the staff members you have contact with at the facility should be able to see a difference in the way you behave. If you are in an outpatient program run by one treatment provider, the treatment provider should be able to see that you've changed.

Types of Workbooks

The Limit & Lead Student Workbook is a type of a workbook known as an "offense-specific" workbook. In other words, this workbook contains therapeutic assignments having to do with your misconduct and behavior that hurt others. Offense-specific treatment is very effective because it can teach you how to stop using harmful behavior.

The other type of workbook used to help individuals with behavior problems is called a "psychoeducational" workbook. These workbooks teach skills like anger management, assertiveness, and social skills. This type of workbook is helpful because it can teach you what to do instead of using the fast-food approach to life.

Using an offense-specific workbook together with a psychoeducational workbook is the best way to help someone stop using harmful behavior. The offense-specific workbook can teach a person what not to do, and the psychoeducational workbook can teach a person what to do. It is a sort of stop-and-go treatment. Hopefully, your treatment provider will supplement this workbook with a psychoeducational workbook.

If you only have time for one type of workbook, use the offense-specific workbook. Hopefully, you won't have to rush through treatment and your treatment provider will supplement this workbook with psychoeducational assignments.

Conclusion

This workbook is not about making you weaker. It is about making you stronger. Use this workbook to learn to control yourself and a lot of good things will happen. You will meet your needs. You will get many of the things you want. You won't have to worry about anyone taking things from you. You will be happy and successful and you will have **No More Victims!**

Help from Adam

A client who successfully completed a treatment program like the one you are in wrote the following about his experience while in treatment. When you read what Adam has to say, think about whether you think the same way. If you don't think like Adam, you may not have the mindset of someone who is a success in treatment. If you don't have the same mindset as Adam, you may want to change the way you think.

It's what I called the "Mental Turning Points IN TREATMENT." It happened when I accepted the fact that I had been CAUGHT. It happened when I accepted the fact that there are PENALTIES for my actions, and that these penalties are APPROPRIATE AND FAIR. It happened when I accepted that I had committed a CRIME against society, my victim, my family, my neighbors, and MYSELF. It happened when I realized that TREATMENT is about HELPING me to find out about myself so that I do not offend again. It happened when I accepted the fact that the TREATMENT rules were good for me and I learned to control my behavior. Once I accepted these FACTS, doing what was required by TREATMENT became very simple and direct. The workbook had a beginning and an end to it. Sometimes these turning points or "modules" that I went through happened quickly or together. Sometimes it took a lot of effort and willpower to overcome FEAR. I remember that, sometimes, my fear of exposure and my fear of punishment kept me from taking steps in the right direction. It is all about ACCEPTING rather than FIGHTING...OPENING rather than CLOSING. Keep in mind that there IS a light at the end of this dark tunnel. In the END I found that I AGREED with the principles of what TREATMENT teaches. It really WORKS!!!

Thinking Errors

Do you cover your mouth before you sneeze? Rumor has it that a sneeze is the fastest action a human can take – yet you can cover your mouth before you sneeze.

What is the most surprising thing about being able to cover your mouth before you sneeze? Is it how fast you can act? No, that is not the most surprising thing.

The most surprising thing about being able to cover your mouth before you sneeze is that you have time to think and plan and act before the sneeze comes. Here is the secret of the sneeze: **You Always Think before You Act!**

Your actions don't just happen. You think and then you act. Even when you have only a little bit of time right before a sneeze, you think before you act. Obviously, if you have to do something more complicated than covering your mouth, you think much longer and deeper before you act.

Since this is a treatment program, you know we wouldn't be talking about sneezes unless it was therapeutic. In order to use the secret of the sneeze to your benefit in treatment, you must stand the secret on its head. If you do that, you come up with an important treatment principle: **if you want to change your behavior, change the way you think.**

Mental health professionals have identified a variety of errors or mistakes in thinking that lead to a variety of mental health problems. Mental health professionals have gotten so good at identifying flawed thinking that this type of thinking is now referred to as "thinking errors."

Thinking errors are the thoughts that you have that lead to criminal behavior. One way that you can begin to stop criminal behavior is to recognize and stop your thinking errors.

Thinking errors mark the way you thought when you were a child. Thinking errors are the perfect formula for the survival of the individual. It just so happens that the survival of the individual based on thinking errors is in conflict with society. Others around you won't be able to meet their needs if you are meeting your needs while using thinking errors. That is why your parents and teachers spent a great deal of time correcting you when you used thinking errors. This process is called socialization.

14

Socialization happens when you learn how to meet your needs in such a way that others can still meet their needs. If you did not follow the training given to you as a child, you still use thinking errors. You need to learn to recognize and control thinking errors. If you can stop using the thinking errors, you will begin taking steps towards the goal of **No More Victims**.

1. POWER PLAY – I know the right way to do things but I don't do things the right way. I do things **my way**. I do whatever I need to do to control people and situations. I abuse my power. I view every situation as win or lose and I will do anything, even wrong or illegal things, to make sure I win.

2. CLOSED CHANNEL – I am close-minded. I do not reveal my true thoughts and feelings. I do not accept feedback from others.

3. SECRETIVENESS – I develop secret relationships with others who I think will help me behave in a criminal way. I develop some secret relationships with people who I plan to hurt using criminal behavior.

4. ENTITLEMENT – I think the world owes me. I think that I am better than others, even though I have done nothing to earn that feeling. I want others to treat me like I am special, and if they don't, I get mad…and I get even. I think that life is unfair if I don't get my way.

5. KEEPING SCORE – I keep track of the times another person confronts me, argues with me, or does me wrong. When I think I can abuse the other person, I attack that person. I try to hurt that person so I can even the score.

6. SELFISHNESS – I do not show care or concern for others. I fail to consider the rights and feelings of others. I do what I want to do, when I want to do it – regardless of whom I hurt. I am selfish when I have the fast-food approach to life.

7. HOP OVER – I do not answer questions when I know the answer would be unpleasant. I hop over the question and answer a different question or change the subject.

8. POOR ME – I try to get others to feel sorry for me. I know that if I can get others to feel sorry for me, I might not get punished for the bad things that I have done. Sometimes I feel sorry for myself so I can justify not following the rules. Sometimes I feel sorry for myself so I can justify doing illegal things.

9. VICTIM STANCE – I try to replace the victim as being the one who was hurt. When I do this, I try to convince others that I was more hurt than the victim was.

10. PET ME – I do things just to get others to praise me. My heart is not in what I am doing. I am just trying to get others to say "good job" or "way to go."

11. MR. GOODGUY/MS. GOODGAL – I wear a mask or false front to hide my criminal thoughts, plans and actions. I mislead others by looking like an ideal and likeable citizen. I pretend that I don't have criminal fantasies, plans, and behaviors but I really do.

12. CONFUSION – I look confused even though I really know what is going on. I try to convince others that I do not know what to do or what is expected of me. I use confusion as an excuse for not doing what I am supposed to do.

13. HELPLESSNESS – I try to make others think that I cannot do what I am asked because I am weak or because I have too much stress in my life. I think if I look helpless, people won't expect much of me.

14. JUSTIFYING – I try to make something wrong appear like it is not wrong.

15. BLAMING – I blame someone or something for causing me to act as I did. I blame others so I can avoid responsibility for my actions.

16. MINIMIZING – I try to make wrong behavior appear small or insignificant. Sometimes I compare my wrong behavior to "worse" behavior so I don't appear to be so bad.

17. MIND-READING – I think that I know what others are thinking. I do not bother to ask other people what they think or what is important to them.

18. ANGER – I let myself get angry easily. I let my anger become intense and I let it spread. I use tantrums and aggression to express anger. When I am angry, I don't think in a normal, rational way, and my anger can lead to criminal acts. Sometimes I use anger to shift the focus from me to something else. I also use anger to seek revenge. Sometimes I get angry, or pretend I am angry, so I can justify hurting someone.

19. SUPER-OPTIMISM – I believe I am so slick and clever that no one will catch me or catch on to my tricks and plans. I think that I won't get caught, or that if I do get caught, I will be able to talk my way out of it.

20. OWNERSHIP – I view others as a possession. I act as if I own the other person. I ignore the other person's feelings and needs. I treat the other person like my personal belonging.

21. MAKING FOOLS OF OTHERS – I make fools of others publicly or in my mind. I exaggerate the mistakes and weaknesses of others to put them down so I can feel superior. If I do this in public, I am trying to raise my status while tearing down another person.

22. CAN'T WAIT – I am impulsive. I do not wait for the proper time to do things. I cannot delay my desires. I do what I want when I want, even if it is not the right time.

23. JAILHOUSE LAWYER – I use legalistic arguments to create a cloud of words to confuse and distract others from what is really relevant. I skillfully focus on rules or morals, and I hide behind them. I divert attention from real issues by focusing on irrelevant, nit-picking details.

24. ZERO STATE – When I feel bored, I feel worthless and empty, like I am nothing. I get the urge to do something illegal or dangerous so I can escape my boredom.

25. UNIQUENESS – I feel I am different and better than others. I think because I am different, the rules that apply to others don't apply to me. I know rules apply to others, but I believe that if people would just realize how special I am, then they would realize that rules don't apply to me.

26. CRIMINAL PRIDE – I take pride in being a criminal. My self-esteem is based on my criminal deeds and accomplishments. Criminal deeds could include criminal offenses or merely breaking rules and feeling proud that I got away with it.

Assignment

1. What is a thinking error?
2. Why is it important to learn to recognize and stop thinking errors?
3. How does a child learn to eliminate thinking errors?
4. Define Power Play.
5. Define Entitlement.
6. Define Selfish.
7. Which thinking errors did you use when you committed your instant offense?
8. Which thinking errors have you used when you have thought about this treatment program?
9. Which thinking errors do you use most often at school? Explain your answer.
10. Which thinking errors do you use most often at home? Explain your answer.

Thought Journal

In order to become skillful at recognizing and stopping thinking errors, you need to start by writing down your thoughts. After you have written down your thoughts, analyze what you wrote. Look for thinking errors.

The thought journal is a way for you to practice finding your thinking errors. After using your thought journal for a period of time, you can develop the skill of catching your thinking errors before you speak or act.

Directions:

1. Your thought journal is like a diary, so you should probably use something like a spiral-bound notebook as your thought journal. Print or use legible handwriting. If your handwriting is not legible, you may be required to type your journal.

2. Make one entry per day. Be sure to write down the date and time of the entry.

3. Write your thoughts for that day. You can write about what you did or things that happened, but **you must always describe what you thought** about these things. Be sure to **write down your thoughts, beliefs, or opinions**.

4. Make sure each entry is five or six sentences long.

5. After you make an entry, read it and find any thinking errors. **List the thinking errors** that you have found in the **left margin**.

6. Complete thought journals on a daily basis. Turn in your thought journals once a week, or more often if your treatment provider requests them.

7. When your treatment provider returns your thought journal, read and think about the feedback from the treatment provider. Consider and be open to all of the feedback, and when a treatment provider directs you to change how you write your thought journal, follow the instructions given by the treatment provider.

8. Continue writing in your thought journal until you are told to stop by your treatment provider.

Sample

In any journal entry, you may mention thoughts, feelings, and actions; however, it is most important to write about your thoughts. In the sample below, the thoughts are in capital letters. Notice how actions and feelings can be included in a journal entry, but thoughts are the most important.

> TODAY WAS A GOOD DAY. I started a new class today. I was a little late but I DON'T THINK ANYONE REALLY CARED. I ate lunch in the cafeteria. I THINK THE FOOD IS LOUSY. THE COOK MUST BE STUPID. After school, I went to group and then went to my room. MY ROOMMATE IS SUCH A MESSY PERSON. I have talked with him several times about keeping the place clean. I DON'T THINK HE CARES. He really makes me angry. I THINK I WILL JUST MESS UP HIS STUFF. I THINK HE DESERVES THAT.

Can you see how it is possible to write your thoughts, feelings, and actions for a particular day? It is also important to be able to recognize the thinking errors. Do you see any thinking errors in the journal entry above? Hint: The phrases written in all-capital letters are thoughts, and there are plenty of thinking errors to be found in these phrases.

Assignment

Begin your thought journal. Make one entry per day and <u>be sure to list your thinking errors in the margin</u>. Give your thought journal to your treatment provider once a week, or more often if requested by your treatment provider.

Criminal Outlets

A criminal outlet is any behavior that lets out a criminal urge. Just like an electrical outlet will let out electricity, a criminal outlet is the way that you let out your criminal urges.

There are two types of criminal outlets: criminal precursors and crimes. A criminal precursor is any behavior that could lead to criminal behavior. A crime is any behavior that breaks the law.

Criminal Outlets: Criminal Precursors

If a behavior is not legally a crime but leads to crime, that behavior is called a "criminal precursor." The word "precursor" means "to come before." Think of criminal precursors as the things that come before a crime. A list of criminal outlets that serve as criminal precursors are presented below:

Lying	*Cheating*	*Selfishness*	*Insulting*
Gossiping	*Cursing*	*Self-indulgence*	*Limit-testing*
Jealousy	*False pride*	*Greed*	*Envy*
Disorderliness	*Hostility*	*Craving*	*Deception/secretiveness*

Remember that criminal precursors are not actual crimes. For example, there are no laws against greed or envy. However, if you let these values guide your behavior, it is only a matter of time before you commit a crime. Since this workbook focuses on prevention, it is important for you to recognize and prevent criminal precursors.

Criminal Outlets: Crime

These outlets are actual crimes. The major categories of crimes are listed. If you can't find a specific crime listed, look for the category that it might fall in.

Theft	*Robbery*	*Perjury*	*Assault*
Murder	*Resisting arrest*	*Sex offenses*	*Use of a weapon*
Fraud	*Escaping/absconding*	*Kidnapping*	*Arson*
Treason	*Vandalism*	*Driving violations*	*Family violence*
Drug-related crimes	*Trespassing*	*Alcohol-related crimes*	*Curfew violations*

Criminal precursors are your early warning system. Criminal precursors warn you that you are on your way to committing a crime. If you catch yourself using criminal precursors, stop yourself. If you can stop a criminal precursor, you can stop yourself from committing a crime. That is something you can be proud of!

Once you become good at using criminal precursors to stop yourself from committing crimes, you should create a new goal for yourself: to stop yourself from using criminal precursors. You create a new victim every time you use a criminal precursor. If you are going to reach the goal of **No More Victims**, you must avoid both types of criminal outlets.

Assignment

1. What is a criminal outlet?
2. What is a criminal precursor?
3. What criminal precursors are you most likely to use?
4. How is a criminal precursor different from a crime?
5. Is it ever okay to have a new victim?
6. Is it possible to commit a crime and not hurt anyone?
7. How can you use criminal precursors to prevent crime?

Criminal vs. Citizen Behavior

You probably thought you were happy and successful when you were committing crimes. Take a look at where you are now: are you as happy and successful as you want to be? Probably not.

How would like to be truly happy and successful? How would like to have a life that you can be proud of, a life in which you don't have to keep secrets or wonder when everyone is going to find out about the last bad thing you did? If you want a life based upon strength and true happiness, try being a citizen. Some definitions are provided below to help you know if you are using citizen or criminal behavior.

Criminal behavior is behavior that meets <u>one or more</u> of the following criteria:

1. You cheat, hurt, harm, or abuse a person, system, organization, company, or community.

2. You fail to show care or concern for the needs and rights of others when meeting your own needs.

3. You believe that you do not need to follow rules because "the world owes me" or "life is unfair."

4. You do dangerous or illegal behavior for thrills or personal gain, or to escape boredom.

Citizen behavior is behavior that meets <u>all</u> of the following criteria:

1. You obey rules, laws and social norms.

2. Your behavior strengthens your relationships with other citizens.

3. Your behavior is valued by other citizens.

Citizens meet their needs, but when they meet their needs they don't interfere with other people meeting their own needs. The criminal is the opposite. When a criminal meets his or her needs, it interferes with other people meeting their own needs.

Since you are in a treatment program that is using this workbook, it should be obvious to you that you were acting like a criminal. You were meeting your needs in a way that kept other people from meeting their own needs. You may have thought that committing a crime was a good way for you to meet your needs, but look at where you are now and ask yourself, "How's that criminal life working out for me now? Do I feel happy? Do I feel successful?" If you are honest, the answer to these questions is "NO!"

If you really want to be happy and successful, behave like a citizen. You should create a "new me" that is based upon citizen thinking, feeling, and behaving. When you act like a citizen, everything you do and all your achievements will be yours. No one can take them away from you. No one will come into your life and take your freedom or the things that you have accumulated. Real happiness and real success is achieved through the power of citizen behavior.

Assignment

1. Which is easier, criminal or citizen behavior? Explain your answer.
2. What is the goal of this program regarding criminal and citizen behavior?
3. How does the goal of this program apply to you?
4. Was your crime citizen or criminal behavior? Explain your answer.
5. Which criteria of criminal behavior did your crime match?
6. Which criteria for citizen behavior did your crime match?
7. Can a crime be both criminal and citizen? Explain your answer.

Honesty

Honesty means telling the truth. In this program, you must be honest about your offense. If you want to be honest about your offense, you have to be honest about two things:

1. **Actions** – You have to be honest about what you did during your offense.
2. **Desires** – You have to be honest that you wanted to commit your offense.

In order to complete this program, you must be honest about your actions and desires. When you are honest about your actions and your desires, you own your offense.

Is it a bad thing to own your offense? Not at all. When you own your offense, a lot of good things happen. Here are some of the good things that happen when you take responsibility for your offense:

1. **Self-Awareness** – When you own your offense, you admit to what you did and why you did it. This means you are getting to know yourself better. When you get to know yourself better, you increase your self-awareness. Self-awareness is the first step in changing yourself.

2. **Secrets** – When you own your offense, you don't have to keep secrets. When you were committing crimes, you kept a lot of secrets about your criminal desires, plans, and behavior. It takes a lot of energy to keep a secret. This is energy that you could have used to enjoy life and be a success. The longer you keep a secret, the more energy you lose. The more energy you lose, the less you enjoy life. If you keep a secret for a long time, you can lose your sense of humor and your ability to concentrate and think. You might even have difficulty eating and sleeping. Secrets are like poison. A secret will poison you until you get it out of your system. You can get secrets and the poison created by secrets out of your system by being honest.

3. **Self-Control** – If you own a problem, you can fix that problem. You can't fix other peoples' problems and other people can't fix your problems. You have to own your problems if you are going to fix your problems. Your past criminal behavior is your problem. Once you own your past criminal behavior, you can start the hard work of fixing that problem so you can reach the goal of **No More Victims!**

Even though there are a lot of good things that can happen when you own your crime, you are probably afraid of being honest. This is natural. No matter what kind of therapy you are in, there is always some fear.

Did you know that depressed people who go to therapy are afraid? You bet they are – every time they go to a therapy session. How about a person who has lost a loved one? Do you think the person in therapy for grief is afraid? Yes, even this person is afraid.

If you are like other people in therapy programs, you will be afraid. The two most common reasons people are afraid in therapy are listed below. Which reason applies to you? Do both reasons apply to you?

1. **Fear of Failure** – You might have difficulty admitting to your problems because you think if you admit to your problems, you will feel like a failure. This is an unrealistic fear because everyone has problems. If you are afraid to admit your problems, you are really afraid to admit you are human. Well, too late – you are human. You do have problems. Everybody knows you are human and everybody knows you have problems. If you don't admit to your problems, you are not fooling anyone…except maybe yourself.

2. **Fear of the Unknown** – You know you have problems, but you are afraid to admit to the problems because if you do, you know you will have to change. Change is scary. If you change, things will be different. Fear of the unknown can be very scary. So, to avoid change, you might just try not admitting to a problem. That way you don't have to change.

It does not matter what type of therapy you are in – you will tell yourself a lot of things to keep yourself from changing. Anything you tell yourself to keep from changing can stop you from being a success. You need to have courage and be honest. You need to make changes. That is the only way to overcome your fear and be happy and successful.

Assignment

1. Are you the kind of person who can admit to his or her faults? Explain your answer.

2. Which is better for you: keeping secrets about your crime or facing your fears and changing? Explain your answer.

3. If you are honest about what you did to your victim, how will that help you?

4. Most people can admit to their criminal behaviors, but they don't want to admit to their desire for the crime. Why is that?

5. How did you hurt yourself by keeping secrets about your crime?

6. What is your biggest fear about being honest about your crime?

How to Change

In this lesson, you will learn about two ways that people change as a result of being in a treatment program: the easy way and the hard way.

Easy Way to Change

The easy way to change is to put yourself in charge of making personal changes. You do this by being honest, by not keeping secrets, and by owning your behavior. If you do these things, you can become happy and successful in three easy steps.

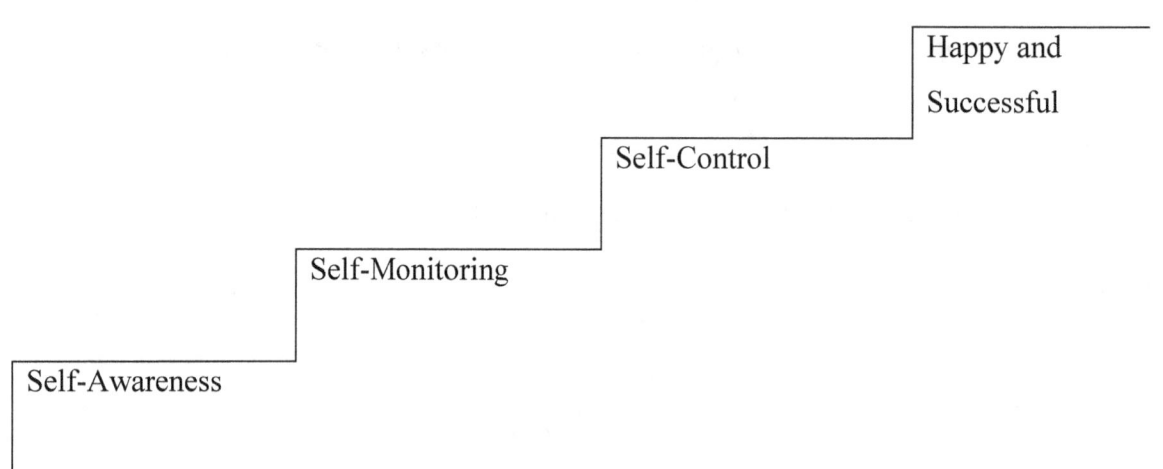

Self-Awareness – You probably know what the word "aware" means. It means to know something. If you are self-aware, you know yourself.

Self-Monitoring – The word "monitor" means to watch. When you self-monitor, you are watching yourself. You must watch yourself to make sure that you don't have criminal thoughts, feelings, and behaviors.

Self-Control – Self-control is being in control of yourself. If you control yourself, you stop your criminal plans, desires, and actions before they happen.

Happy and Successful – If you can take the first three steps, you will feel good about yourself and you will be a success.

If you want to change, the first step is to know yourself. The second step is to watch for things that show you are about to do something bad. The third step is to control yourself when you feel like doing something bad. If you do these three steps, you will make it to the last step. You will be happy and successful.

The Hard Way to Change

If you are like a lot of other clients who have used this workbook, it wasn't your idea to use this workbook. Someone is probably making you use this workbook, and you resent that – so you are doing all you can to not change. What you don't know is that you will change. You will just do it the hard way:

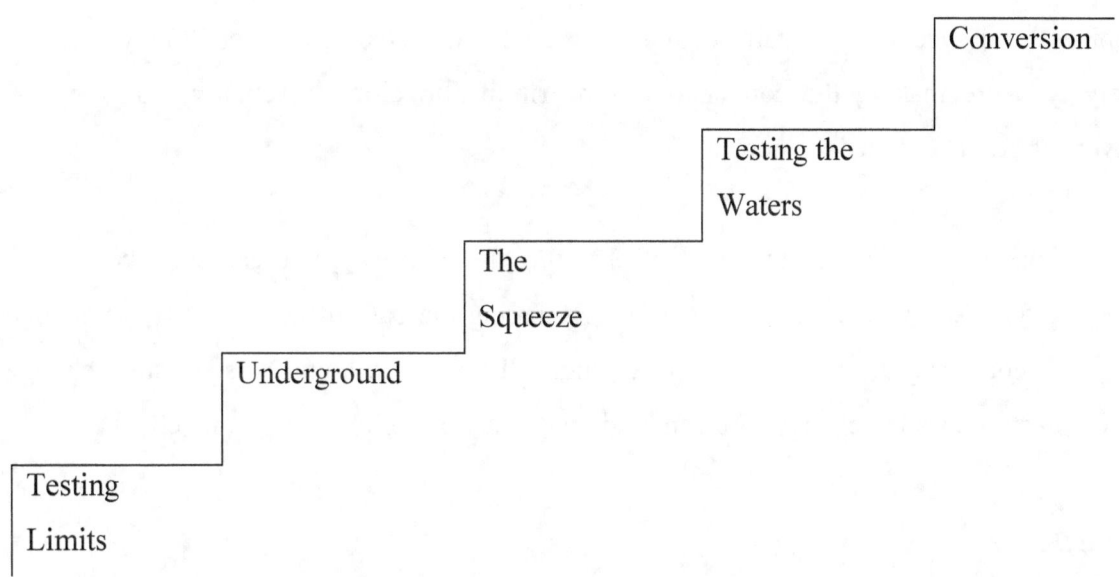

Testing Limits – If someone forced you into this treatment program, you are resentful. You hate it and you let everyone know you hate being here by breaking rules, not doing assignments, and challenging those trying to help you.

Underground – After you have been punished enough times for testing limits, you get tired of the punishment – so you get sneaky. You go underground. You appear to be following rules when others are around, but when they aren't, you are back to your old criminal ways.

The Squeeze – The squeeze happens after you have gotten caught being sneaky. Sometimes you have to be caught many, many times being sneaky, but eventually you learn that you are not as slick as you think, and people can tell you are "underground." You realize that being underground isn't safe, so you have to find a different safe place.

Testing the Waters – You aren't safe when you are underground, so you decide to test the waters by trying to do something that a citizen might do. But you tell yourself you are only go to do one thing, and if it doesn't work, you are going back to the "old me."

Conversion – After you test the waters and figuring out that being a citizen leads to happiness and success, you start behaving more and more like a citizen. Slowly but surely, you are making the conversion from criminal to citizen. Actually, you are converting from "old me" to "new me."

Once you go through the steps of changing the hard way, you can start the steps of changing the easy way. Yes, that is correct. By taking the path of the hard way to change, you were not doing the real work of changing. All you were doing was resisting change. Once you stop resisting change, you can begin the real work of changing yourself.

Assignment

1. Why does it take longer to finish this treatment program if you take the hard path first?
2. Which path to change do you think you will take: easy or hard? Explain your answer.
3. If you know you are on the path of the hard way to change, which step are you on? How will you get off that step?

Why Should I Change?

Making personal change is difficult. If you don't have a good reason for changing, you will probably have difficulty changing. In fact, you might not change at all.

Changing from criminal to citizen is a lot easier when you know it is good for you. Let's take a look at some of the good things that will happen to you if you do change.

1. **Lasting Happiness** – Using criminal outlets was probably fun and exciting but did it bring you lasting happiness? Look at yourself right now. If you are honest, you will have to say that criminal outlets did not bring you lasting happiness. If you want lasting happiness, you can't use criminal outlets. If you want fun, excitement and lasting happiness, you have to use citizen behavior.

2. **Detox** – Living a criminal lifestyle is like swimming in pool of toxic chemicals; it can make you sick, and in the end, it just might kill you. If you change from criminal to citizen, it is like using a ladder to climb out of that pool of toxic chemicals. Once you are out of the pool of toxic chemicals, you can start to heal.

3. **Paranoia** – What was it like wondering if you would be caught for your last criminal act? It did not even have to be your last criminal act – any one of your criminal acts can lead to loss of freedom. Did you spend a lot of time worrying and waiting to get caught? Guess what? Citizens don't have to worry. They can spend their time and energy having fun.

4. **True Power** – You probably thought you had true power when you were committing crimes, but you didn't. True power can stand the test of time. The things you gained using criminal power don't last. Everything you got by using criminal outlets can be taken from you. The things that a citizen gets are his or hers forever. Even if a criminal takes something from a citizen, the law works to return the citizen's belongings. True power is based on citizen power, not criminal power.

The benefits listed above are just a few of the benefits of changing. If you make the change from criminal to citizen, you will probably experience all of the benefits listed above, and other benefits that are not even on the list. For example, do you think you will proud of yourself if you change? If the answer is yes, then that is an additional benefit. Will your mother or father be proud of you if you change? That could be another benefit for you.

It is also important to keep in mind that if you change, you will reach the goal of this program: **No More Victims**! You probably created a lot of victims in your past. You owe it to yourself, your family, friends and community to have **No More Victims**!

Assignment

1. If you are a success, who will know about your success – family, friends, group members, supervising officer?

2. If you are a success, what will the people in item #1 above think about you? How did they think about you when you weren't a success?

3. If you are a success, how will you feel? What will you think of yourself?

4. Future Essay: write a three-paragraph essay about how your life will be when you are a success in this program and you are living like a citizen.

Thinking Leads to Emotions and Behavior

Your thoughts determine how you feel. Your thoughts and feelings together determine how you act.

Most people believe that an event leads to an emotion: event → emotion. This is not true. You can give yourself a test right now. Suppose you are watching a basketball game. You are rooting for one team, the Bulls, and your friend is rooting for the other team, the Hawks. How will you feel if your team wins? How will your friend feel if your team wins? If you said that you would feel good if your team won and your friend would feel sad if your team won, you would be correct. But take a look at what you are saying. You are saying that one event can cause two different emotions.

If events do not cause emotions, what does cause emotions? Simple – it is the way you think about events that causes emotions. When your team wins, you think it is a good thing. When your team wins, your friend thinks it is a bad thing. The feelings you and your friend have depend on what you each think.

Event	Thought	Emotion
Bulls win →	I'm a Bulls fan. I like that. →	Happy
Bulls win →	I'm not a Bulls fan. I don't like that. →	Sad

This is pretty neat information, but how can you use it for your benefit? Easy – if you don't like the way you feel, change the way you think. If you change the way you think, you can change the way you feel.

Let's take a look at your current situation. You are being asked to complete a treatment program that you probably didn't volunteer for. You could react to this event with resentment, feeling anger. On the other hand, you could think of this treatment program as an opportunity. It might just be the beginning of a new life full of happiness and success.

Event	Thought	Emotion
I'm in this program $\rightarrow$	No one can tell me what to do. It's not fair. $\rightarrow$	Anger
I'm in this program $\rightarrow$	I deserve to be here. I need to make the most of it. I don't want to lose again. $\rightarrow$	Happy

In this program, you will be talking about an analyzing your thoughts because your thoughts are the basis for your feelings and actions. If you want to change the way you feel or the way you behave, you have to change the way you think. In other words, you have to develop self-control over your thinking. If you have self-control over your thinking, you can control your emotions and your behavior.

Assignment

1. Do events cause emotions?
2. How do thoughts cause emotions?
3. Why is happiness a choice?
4. What thoughts do you need to change right now to be happier?

34

The Why Sandwich

One reason why you might be in this program is that you have poor problem solving skills. If you are not good at solving problems, you can get caught up in a lot of problems. You might feel like you can never win or like you will never be rid of your problems.

There is good news. Even if you are not good at solving problems, you can change. You can learn how to become a good problem solver. There are two basic rules to solving a problem:

1. **Don't Add to Your Problems.** When you solve a problem, your solution should make the problem go away. If your solution creates more problems, you have added to your problems. This is not good problem solving. For example, pretend that you broke a treatment rule and pretend that your treatment provider asks you if you broke the rule. It would be smart to admit to breaking the rule. It would not be smart to lie. If you lie, you add to your problems – first you had the problem of breaking a rule, and now you have the problem of telling a lie.

2. **Be direct.** Don't try to ignore a problem. Don't try to wait until the problem disappears. Don't pretend that the problem does not exist. Deal directly with the problem. Deal with your problems sooner rather than later.

The "Why Sandwich" method is a problem solving skill. It is simple. You can use the Why Sandwich to deal directly with your problems. You can use it during therapy sessions. You can even use the Why Sandwich at school, home, or work, or in personal relationships.

Here are three steps in the Why Sandwich method. The first step is a "what" question: *"What is the problem?"* The second question is a "why" question: *"Why is it a problem?"* The final question is another "what" question: *"What am I going to do about it?"*

The name of this method for solving problems is called the Why Sandwich because there is one "Why" question sandwiched in between two "What" questions.

What: What is the Problem?

In this step of the problem-solving process, you must define the who, what, when, and where of the problem. If you do a good job of defining the problem, a solution might suggest itself.

What is the problem?	Where did it happen?
Who is involved?	How many times has it happened?
When did it happen?	How did it start?
How did it happen?	Who knows about the problem?

Why: Why is it a problem?

If you understand why something is a problem, it can create motivation for you to solve the problem. Understanding why something is a problem can also help you understand why other people are concerned about the problem.

Why is it a problem?	Why do others think it is a problem?
Are other people hurt?	Is it part of a cycle?
Why is it a problem for me?	How does it hurt me and others?

What: What am I going to do about the problem?

It is okay to rely on others for help with your problem, but remember that this is your problem and you should be the one who does most of the work to overcome the problem.

What can I do?	How can I prevent the problem in the future?
Can anyone help me?	What have other people done in a similar situation?

Assignment

Get a piece of paper and use the Why Sandwich to solve one of the problems you are experiencing at this time in your life.

ACE: Self-Control Techniques

Even if you want to switch from a criminal lifestyle to a citizen lifestyle, you may still be tempted to go back to the "old me" way of behaving. Don't worry if you are tempted. Anybody trying to overcome a bad habit will be tempted to use the bad habit.

If you want to make the change from "old me" to "new me," you should do what other people have done when they successfully quit a bad habit. You should play the "ACE."

ACE stands for Avoid, Cope, and Escape. If you find yourself being tempted to act like a criminal, you play the ACE. You avoid, cope, or escape.

Some situations are more tempting than others. Situations that are very tempting are called high-risk situations. A high-risk situation is any person, place, or thing that makes it easier for you to use a criminal outlet. A high-risk situation doesn't cause you to use a criminal outlet, it just makes using a criminal outlet easier. You still have to choose to use the criminal outlet. Crime is always a choice.

If you want to successfully deal with every high-risk situation, you have to play the ACE. Below are some instructions on how you can play the ACE.

Avoid – You use the self-control technique of avoidance by staying away from high-risk situations. You must be <u>smart</u> enough to know the people, places, and things that are high-risk for you, and you must be <u>strong</u> enough to stay away.

Cope – You use coping self-control techniques on your thoughts and feelings. The feelings most likely to lead to crime are unpleasant emotions: anger, fear, or sadness. The thoughts most likely to lead to crime are criminal urges and temptation. The most effective way to deal with anger, fear, sadness, urges, and temptation is to use one of the coping techniques listed below.

1. **<u>Tunnel Vision</u>** – When you find yourself in a high-risk situation, do not pay attention to the person or thing that is making it easier for you to use a criminal outlet. Instead, focus on citizen thoughts and actions. This technique gets its name because you narrow your

attention, like looking down a tunnel narrows what you can see. For example, imagine you are riding in a car. You see an old friend you used to do drugs with. He sees you. He waves at you. You turn your head away and look straight ahead and don't acknowledge him. As you drive by, you think about all the positive things in your life that you now have because you are living a citizen lifestyle.

2. **Thought Broadcasting** – If you get an urge to use a criminal outlet, imagine that your thought is being broadcast from your mind over a loudspeaker. Imagine that as your thought is broadcast, people turn and look at you and respond to what they hear you broadcasting. You decide to stop thinking about the criminal outlet because people are getting mad at you for having those thoughts. You begin to fear that you might get into trouble. You stop what you are thinking, so you can avoid any problems.

3. **Reality Check** – When you get an urge to use a criminal outlet, conduct a reality check by asking yourself questions: *"How realistic is that I could use this criminal outlet and get away with it? What kind of trouble could I get into if I actually tried to do what I am thinking? Is this citizen or criminal behavior? If I want lasting happiness and true power, I should act like a citizen – is this acting like a citizen?"* Let reality be your guide as you make yourself stop thinking about behavior that could lead to you losing your freedom.

4. **Reversal** – If you catch yourself having a criminal urge, imagine a person that you don't like having the same urges towards you. For example, let's say you don't like really tall men with dark hair and dark eyes. You need to imagine this man having the exact same criminal urge towards you. You can even imagine him coming up to you and talking to you. Imagine that he is talking to you about the weather but underneath you know he really wants to harm you.

   Another way to do reversal is to imagine someone you don't like having a criminal urge toward someone you love. For example, imagine someone you don't like is having the same harmful urge you are having except they are having the urge towards your sister, brother, mother, etc. Let the negative images you get from this cause your criminal urge to disappear.

5. **Golden Rule** – When you notice that you are having a criminal urge, consider whether this urge helps you reach the goal of **No More Victims**. If the urge can lead to more victims, tell yourself to change your thoughts. You can also consider whether or not this type of urge is good for you and for those you love. If you think that this urge might cause you or your loved ones problems, you must change your thoughts.

Escape – You use the self-control technique of escape by leaving a high-risk situation. Sometimes, you may unexpectedly find yourself in a high-risk situation. For example, quite by accident you may come in contact with a person, place, or thing that you know could lend itself easily to criminal behavior. You must be <u>strong and smart</u>. You must leave.

Assignment

Get a notebook, and on the first page, write the names of all of the ACE techniques, including the five coping techniques. As you go through your day, monitor yourself. Each time you come in contact with a high-risk situation, write a brief description of the situation and list the self-control technique you used, whether it is one of the coping techniques, or avoidance or escape. At the end of the day, let your treatment provider see your log. It is pretty common for treatment providers to ask clients to do this assignment for about a week.

Your Role as a Member of the Treatment Team

As a client in this treatment program, your goal is to switch to a citizen lifestyle. You are trying to transform from the "old me," who used to commit crimes, to the "new me," who lives a citizen lifestyle. The role you should play in this treatment program is that of the "new me."

There are at least three other types of individuals who are involved in your treatment, and you need to know the roles of everyone involved.

- **Staff Members/Supervising Officer** – If you are in a residential program, like detention or a halfway house, the staff members are part of your treatment team. If you are in the community, your supervising officer is part of your treatment team. All staff members and supervising officers have the same job: they make sure you get feedback on whether you are living a citizen lifestyle. If you aren't living a citizen lifestyle, they will encourage you to change. If you don't change, it is their job to report you to the court or parole board. You might get into more trouble if that that happens.

- **Treatment Provider** – Your treatment provider will be using this workbook to help you create your "new me."

- **Support Group** – If you are going to permanently change from the "old me" to the "new me," you need the help of your loved ones. Your loved ones, like parents, brothers, and sisters, should be part of your treatment team, if they are not high-risk individuals. Remember, a high-risk individual is anyone who makes it easier for you to choose to use a criminal outlet. If your parents and siblings are high-risk, you might have to find other family or friends to be part of your treatment team.

While you are working on switching from the "old me" to the "new me," your treatment team will try to help by teaching you how to be a citizen, encouraging you to be a citizen, and giving you a feedback on the amount and type of change they can see in you.

Your support group is more important than you may realize, because during your lifetime, you will have more contact with your support group than you will ever have with your treatment provider, staff members, or supervising officers. You need to create your support group when you begin treatment. You need to keep your support group involved throughout your treatment. When you get out of treatment, you need to remain close to your support group. In the end, much of your success in treatment will be determined by how much help your support group gives you.

Assignment

1. What is your role as a member of your treatment team?

2. What role does your treatment provider play as part of your treatment team?

3. What role does the supervision or monitoring staff play as part of your treatment team?

4. What is a support group?

5. What role does your support group play as part of your treatment team?

6. Which family or friends do you think should be part of your treatment team?

7. Which family or friends do you think should NOT be part of your treatment team?

Module Two: Honesty about Your Criminal Behavior

In the Orientation Module, you learned a lot of new things. Now it is time to see if you can use those things to change from the "old me" to the "new me." The assignments in this module will challenge you to use what you learned so you can be honest about your instant offense and your criminal history.

Your instant offense is the offense for your most recent conviction or adjudication. When you are honest about your instant offense, you admit to two things: your actions and the thoughts and feelings that led to your actions.

Most clients have an easy time admitting to their actions. It is much more difficult to admit to the thoughts and feelings that led to the actions. When you admit to the thoughts and feelings that led to your actions it is like saying, *"Yeah, I wanted to hurt that guy,"* or *"Yeah, I wanted to act like a criminal."* It is much easier to say, *"I acted like a criminal"* than to say, *"I thought and felt like a criminal."* But your crime didn't just happen. You had to think before you acted.

Some people try to escape being honest by saying that their crime was an accident or was somebody else's fault. You cannot say that your offense was an accident. You cannot blame the victim. You cannot make excuses like, *"It just happened"* or *"I was high. I didn't know what I was doing."* You have to admit that your crime was the result of your ideas, plans, and desires.

The level of honesty you will have to show in order to be honest about your offense will probably be unlike anything you have ever done in the past. You need to be more honest than at any time in your life. When you are done with the assignments about being honest about your instant offense, you will have to be honest about your criminal history.

You might be wondering why you are being challenged to be honest about your criminal history. The reason is simple: if you are going to use self-control to make sure you don't use criminal outlets, you have to identify your personal pattern of using criminal outlets. Once you take a close look at your instant offense and your criminal history, you will see things about your behavior that you never saw before.

Help from Ben

Ben was in a program very similar to the one you are in right now. At the time Ben wrote this, Ben had completed many assignments, but he wasn't quite done with treatment. Eventually, Ben completed treatment and he was happy that he did.

I think understanding that everything in your workbook pertains to something in your life is the biggest part of treatment. If you don't understand it, you have to ask questions. If don't, you don't get anywhere.

I've asked a lot of stupid questions. Lord knows I have, but the response I got helped for whatever situation I faced.

You have to work very hard at every assignment to get through it. A lot of them are difficult to do, but don't get discouraged. You'll get good feedback, and if there is something that you don't understand, ask. That is the biggest way to receive and give help.

Don't think that doing a poor job on a particular assignment will get you by because it won't. You have to work hard at it if you want to get further along. You have to be honest in everything you write.

Just remember that understanding why you're here and why you want to succeed is entirely up to you.

Ben is right. If you want to succeed, you will have to be honest and you will have to work hard. In the end, it comes down to one thing: do you know what you want to gain from working on assignments from this workbook? Well, do you know? What kind of person will you be when you finish this workbook? Will you be the same? Will you be different? One thing is certain – you will be exactly who you really want to be. It is not a matter of which assignments you do. It is a matter of how you use the assignments to make a difference in your life.

My Thoughts before My Instant Offense

Crime does not just happen. You have to think about a crime before you can commit a crime. In fact, there are three thoughts that you have to have before you commit a crime: urge, fantasy, and plan. Even before the crime happens, you start transforming these thoughts into action by the way you set up the situation so you can commit the crime.

Urge $\rightarrow$ **Fantasy** $\rightarrow$ **Plan** $\rightarrow$ **Set-Up** $\rightarrow$ **Crime** $\rightarrow$ **Consequence**

Urge – A criminal urge happens when you feel like committing a crime. Sometimes an urge feels like excitement, like when you are thinking about getting money from selling drugs. Sometimes an urge feels like anger, like when you are thinking about getting revenge.

Fantasy – A fantasy is a mental picture plus a feeling. In a fantasy leading up to committing a crime, the mental picture will be a picture of you committing the crime. The feeling you get is also part of the fantasy. Normally, you feel happy, excited, or satisfied when you have a mental image of yourself committing a crime.

Plan – When you plan, you consider different ways to make your fantasy come true. The plan that you use depends on the type of fantasy you are having. Some plans are simple: wait until nobody is looking. Other plans are complex: come up with a specific time, place, and manner of committing the crime.

Set-Up – The set-up is anything that you do to make sure you can commit the crime and escape. Sometimes a set up simple: break into the building late at night when no one is there. Sometimes a set-up is complex: meet with the owner of the building, establish trust, and have him tell you the security code for the alarm system.

Crime – The crime breaks the law but it is also creates strong emotions in you. Often you feel intense excitement and happiness.

Consequence – As you know, the consequence you received for your crime was negative. You got caught and were punished.

The good news is that you thought before you committed any of your crimes. That is good news because the amount of time you spent fantasizing and planning your crime is the amount of time that you have to stop yourself. Because you think before you act, you have a chance to stop yourself before your criminal thoughts turn into criminal acts.

You have probably heard some individuals say that they didn't plan their crime. They say that their crime just happened. That is not true but let's pretend it is true. Let's pretend that there is such a person who can act without thinking. Do you know what we would call this person? We would call this person the "most dangerous person on earth."

If an individual can commit a crime without thinking, this means that individual is so impulsive that he doesn't have any warning he is about to act out. He is the most dangerous kind of person because he can't stop himself.

Don't say that your crime just happened or that you didn't think or plan before you committed your crime. It makes you sound like the most dangerous type of person. Do yourself a favor: use your self-awareness when answering questions about your offense, and be honest about the thoughts and feelings you had before you committed your crime.

Assignment

1. What urges did you have before you committed your instant offense?
2. What fantasy did you have before you committed your instant offense?
3. What planning did you do before you committed your instant offense?
4. What did you do to set up the instant offense?
5. Why is it a bad thing to say you didn't think about your crime before you did it?

The Way that I Felt about My Instant Offense

A person seeks pleasure and avoids pain – that is human nature. You followed that simple rule any time that you committed a crime. You used the criminal behavior that got you into this program because you thought that it would make you feel good.

There are a lot of ways that criminal behavior can make a person feel good, but feeling good about something does not make it right. A lot of wrong things can feel good. A criminal act is something that can make you feel good but is a bad thing to do. Here are some of the ways that a criminal act can make a person feel good:

1. **Gratification** – If you are honest with yourself, all the things leading up to your instant offense, and the crime itself, were probably exciting. You probably felt some happiness and a feeling of success when you committed your crime. These are the ways that your instant offense could be gratifying.

2. **Relief** – Your offense could have been a way of releasing stress. When you committed your offense, you could have experienced relief from stress.

3. **Power** – Some people who commit crimes get a feeling of power and control when committing crimes. For these people, feeling powerful and being in control are very exciting and enjoyable experiences.

4. **Revenge** – Sometimes, a criminal act is actually an act of revenge. For example, if someone does you wrong, you can get revenge by hurting that person. After you hurt the other person, your revenge will be satisfied and you will feel happy.

This list does not cover all the possibilities. But you don't have to worry about all the possibilities – you just have to worry about the reasons that *you* thought *your* instant offense would feel good.

Assignment

1. What was the most exciting or enjoyable part of your offense?
2. Why did you commit your act – gratification, relief, power, revenge, or some combination of these things?

My Fantasies about the Victim

A crime is an interpersonal event. In other words, a crime happens between two or more people. One of the people involved in the crime is the criminal. The others involved in the crime are the victims.

Some people like to pretend that there are such things as victimless crimes. This is not true; there is no such thing as a victimless crime. For example, a drug dealer might want to say there is no victim when he sells drugs. After all, the person who bought the drug wanted to buy the drug. No matter how you look at it, the person buying the drugs is a victim. Any harm that happens to the victim because of drugs can be traced back to the drug dealer. No matter the crime, there is always a victim.

You thought about your victim before you committed your crime. In fact, you could have had one or more of the thoughts listed below when thinking about your victim:

1. **Mutual Enjoyment** – You think that the victim will enjoy the offense as much as you do. This is common in drug deals and prostitution.

2. **Shock and Fear** – You think that the victim will experience shock and fear, and you find this exciting.

3. **Victim Has Insurance** – You tell yourself stealing from a business is not like stealing form an individual. After all, the business has insurance and anything you take, insurance will replace.

4. **First Blood** – You tell yourself the person you are about to victimize hurt you first. You tell yourself that if that person had not hurt you, you wouldn't have to hurt that person. They drew first blood, and all you are doing is reacting.

5. **No One Is Home** – This is common in home burglaries. You tell yourself that since no one is home, no one is hurt.

Don't be surprised if you had more than one of the fantasies listed above. Also, don't be surprised if you had fantasies about your crime that are not listed above. The list above is not supposed to be a complete list – it is just a list to help you remember the fantasies that you had about your crime.

Assignment

1. Which of the fantasies listed above did you have about your victim? Explain your answer – give some detail about your fantasies.

2. Are there any fantasies you had about your victim that are not listed above? Explain your answer.

My Double Life

When you were busy committing crimes, you tried to appear like you were not committing crimes. You tried to convince everyone that you were a citizen – but this was a false front. Behind this false front, there was the mind and heart of a criminal, and when no one was looking, you committed your crimes. You were living a double life.

Living a double life happens when you behave one way when there are people around and you behave another way when it is just you and your partners in crime. You used your double life to commit crimes. You used your double life to make sure no one would know what you were doing.

It is time to reveal your double life. There are two reasons to do this. First, it will be a good way for your family and friends to get to know just how criminal you used to be. Once your family and friends know about your double life, they will be able to help you stop living a double life. You will be safe and you will feel successful.

Second, when you reveal your double life, you will control it. When the secret of your double life is revealed, your double life can no longer control you. You have a much better chance of reaching the treatment goal of **No More Victims** if you rid yourself of your secrets.

DOUBLE LIFE WITH YOUR VICTIM

1. Identify the victim your instant offense.
2. Why did you have to have a double life with your victim?
3. How did you create and maintain a double life with your victim?
4. Give at least five examples, conversations, interactions, or situations that describe or reveal how you used your double life with your victim.

DOUBLE LIFE WITH YOUR FAMILY

5. Identify one family member who was a victim of your double life.
6. Why did you have to use a double life with this family member?
7. How did you create and maintain a double life with this family member?

8. Give at least five examples, conversations, interactions, or situations that describe or reveal how you used your double life with this family member.

DOUBLE LIFE WITH YOUR FRIENDS

9. Identify one friend who was a victim of your double life.

10. Why did you have to have a double life with this friend?

11. How did you create and maintain a double life with this friend?

12. Give at least five examples, conversations, interactions, or situations that describe or reveal how you used your double life with this friend.

Offense Summary Worksheet

In this assignment, you will be asked to be honest about your instant offense. In order to be honest about your instant offense, you will need to be honest about everything that led up to your offense, and about what you did when you committed your offense.

There are rewards for being honest about your instant offense. First, you will increase your self-awareness. This is the first step in changing yourself. Second, when you are honest, you will reveal secrets. Secrets are like poison. Secrets make you sick. When you write about your secrets, you will feel better.

Do not let fear stop you from being honest. You will be tempted to hide information about your offense. Don't do this. This will only make your treatment more difficult. Not only that, it will make treatment longer. Be honest. Be a success.

Assignment

1. **What were the date and time of your instant offense?**

   Your instant offense is your offense of most recent conviction or adjudication. Give the date and time for your instant offense. Be specific. Give the day, month and year. Give the time of day.

2. **Who was the victim of your instant offense?**

   Give the person's first name, age at the time of the instant offense, relationship to you, and how you knew the victim. If there is more than one victim, list all the victims.

3. **Who was harmed by your offense?**

   There are three levels of victims: *primary* (the victim), *secondary* (victim's family and friends and your family and friends), and *tertiary* or *third* (society and others who know about the offense). You need to consider that you yourself may or may not be a victim.

4. **When was the first time that you thought about committing your offense?**

   You had to think about your crime before you committed your crime. If you want to get control over your criminal behavior, you will have to trace your instant offense back to the very first time you thought about committing your crime. Remember that the longer you plan a crime, the longer you have to stop yourself. In other words, don't say that your crime just happened or that you didn't think about it, because you will be saying you are so impulsive that you are the most dangerous type of person in the world.

5. **How did you feel and what did you think when you were planning your crime?**

   Be sure to write about your emotions – were you happy, sad, mad, or scared when you thought about committing your crime? Also, what were you thinking? You might want to refer to the previous assignment, "*The Way I Felt about My Instant Offense.*"

6. **How did you fantasize that the victim would respond to your crime?**

   What mental picture did you have about how the victim would react? What emotions did you fantasize the victim would have? You might want to refer to the previous assignment, "*My Fantasies about the Victim.*"

7. **Describe how you set up the victim.**

   When you set up a victim, you create a situation in which you can commit the crime and escape. Describe how you set up the victim and any people who could have stopped you. Also describe how you set up the environment, e.g., did you wait until dark; wait until no one was around, etc.? You might want to refer to the previous assignment, "*My Double Life.*"

8. **Describe what you did to the victim.**

   Write a story with a beginning, middle, and end. In the beginning of the story, write about your planning and how you set up the victim and others. The middle part of the story should talk about the crime. The ending of the story should be about how you were caught and the price you had to pay.

Help from Chance

Chance was a very secretive person before he got into therapy. Since being in therapy, he has admitted to how much he used to lie. He likes being honest. This is what he has to say about honesty:

I am an offender and I am in treatment. I have found out that if I am not honest, I will not get out of treatment. I also figured out that if I am not honest, I will be the same person, and I don't want to be that person anymore.

I have learned that honesty is the best way of being a good citizen — but that is not all. I have learned about myself. I have learned how to make use of the tools in treatment. The more I learn about myself, the more I like myself, and the more I like myself, the more I can care for other people.

My life is much easier. The reason is honesty. When you are not honest with someone, it will work you. With my mother, I told her I did not do my crime. It wore on me. I rode it for a week. I left group. I got into my car and went down the road. I told my mother that I did it. She said, "I knew it all along." I made myself sick not telling her something that she already knew. Honesty is easy. Secrets make you sick.

I am not dirt. I am not going to get pushed around. I am doing something good for myself. I am in therapy. I deserve good things. Keep in mind you are a good person. A bad person would not be in group. A bad person would still be out there offending. You are a good person. Never forget it.

What I Learned about Myself from My Offense Summary Worksheet

As a result of completing treatment assignments, you are supposed to be different. In fact, some of the biggest changes in treatment come in the first part of treatment.

In this assignment, you will take stock of the ways you have changed. Get some input from the important people in your life, and be sure to give yourself credit where you deserve it.

1. **What do you know about yourself that you did not know before you began treatment?**

   Don't just look at one or two of the assignments that you have done. Give yourself credit for all the work you have done on all the assignments, including those in the Orientation Module. Don't forget to think about the things that you learned in group therapy sessions, e.g., listening to others present worksheets, listening to educational lessons, etc.

2. **What are some of the good things that you have learned about yourself?**

   If you are going to be a success in life, you need to know what your strengths are. Be objective and give yourself credit for the good things about you and the good things that you do.

3. **What are some of the things that you learned about yourself that you do not like?**

   If you are going to be successful, you need to know what your weak points are. What things do you think, feel, or do that you wish you could change? Are you still a work in progress? If so, what are the things that you are working on?

4. **How has your thinking changed?**

   Your thinking can include urges, fantasies, plans, and thinking errors. Have you made changes in any of these areas? Do you think about yourself and other people differently?

5. **How has the way you deal with your emotions changed?**

   Are you as sad, angry, or fearful as you used to be? Are you happier? If your emotions have changed, why do you think they have changed?

6. **Has the way that you deal with people changed?**

   What you learn in treatment should make a difference in the way you behave outside of treatment. This is particularly true for your relationships. Has treatment made a difference in the way that you interact with others? Explain how you have changed.

Criminal History Questionnaire

In this assignment, you will be challenged to reveal all of the criminal behavior that you have done in your entire life. This assignment is difficult, but not because you will have trouble recalling everything that you did. This assignment is difficult because of the amount of honesty that you must use to complete it.

You are being asked to do this assignment because it is necessary. When you reveal your criminal history, you and your treatment provider get important information. Your criminal history reveals the pattern of your criminal behavior. Once you can see this pattern, you will know what you must control. Remember, this program is all about you learning self-control so someone else, like law enforcement, doesn't come in and control you.

Chronological Order: When answering an item, go in chronological order. For example, when you are answering the question about your drug- and alcohol-related offenses, start with the first offense you committed. Then list the second, and keep listing them in order from first to last. If you complete your list of offenses and remember something that needs to go on the list, don't just put it at the end of the list. Put it in the correct chronological order.

Fifth Amendment Right: You have the right to avoid self-incrimination. You have the right to not testify against yourself. Anything you say, do, or write in treatment can end up in court, and it can be used against you, so do not give information that would result in a legal charge against you. This means that when you are completing this assignment, you should not give the name of any victims or the location, date, or time of any arrestable behavior. The criminal history assignment is designed to help you and your treatment provider discover your pattern of criminal behavior, so treatment can be individualized and effective. Since your treatment provider is not conducting a criminal investigation, you don't need to provide him or her with the kinds of details that would result in a new criminal charge against you. Protect yourself. Do not say, do, or write details that will result in a legal charge against you.

Obligation to Report: Reporting laws vary from state to state; however, most states require that a treatment provider report certain types of suspected criminal behavior. For this reason, you need to make sure that you protect yourself by using your Fifth Amendment Right.

Be honest when you answer these questions. The more open and honest you are, the more likely you are to get the help that you need.

1. **Theft** – Have you ever attempted to commit or actually committed theft? Included in this item behavior such as stealing, breaking and entering, burglary of a building, burglary of a habitation, possession of stolen goods, possession of goods obtained through crime, shoplifting, and/or auto theft. Fifth Amendment Right – Do not reveal the name(s) of the victim(s) or the location, date, or time of any crimes.

2. **Robbery** – Have you ever attempted or engaged in robbery? Robbery occurs when you have face-to-face contact with the victim. Include in this item robbery, armed robbery, robbery with injury, and/or extortion. Fifth Amendment Right – Do not reveal the name(s) of the victim(s) or the location, date, or time of any crimes.

3. **Alcohol- & Drug-Related Crimes**: Have you ever attempted or engaged in drug- or alcohol-related crimes? Include in this item possession of a controlled substance, sale or delivery of drugs, importing drugs, possession of drug paraphernalia, growing crops that could be turned into drugs, manufacturing drugs, giving drugs or alcohol to a minor, use of inhalants, minor in possession of alcohol, public intoxication, and/or driving while intoxicated. Fifth Amendment Right – Do not reveal the name(s) of the victim(s) or the location, date, or time of any crimes.

4. **Assault & Family Violence**: Have you ever attempted or engaged in assault? Include in this definition simple assault, physical assault, assault with bodily injury, assault with a weapon, family violence, stalking, aggravated assault, and/or terroristic threat. Fifth Amendment Right – Do not reveal the name(s) of the victim(s) or the location, date, or time of any crimes.

5. **Use or Possession of Weapons**: Have you ever used or possessed an illegal weapon? Include in this item use or possession of an illegal knife, handgun, rifle, explosive,

club, bat, and/or martial arts weapon. <u>Fifth Amendment Right</u> – Do not reveal the name(s) of the victim(s) or the location, date, or time of any crimes.

6. **Sexual Offense**: Have you ever attempted or completed a sex offense? Include in this item rape, child molestation, date rape, indecent exposure, voyeurism (peeping Tom), prostitution, pimping, touching or bumping without permission, bestiality, and/or obscene phone calls. <u>Fifth Amendment Right</u> – Do not reveal the name(s) of the victim(s) or the location, date, or time of any crimes.

7. **Driving Offense**: Have you ever attempted or completed a driving offense? Include in this item hit and run, reckless driving, road rage driving, and/or leaving the scene of an accident/crime. <u>Fifth Amendment Right</u> – Do not reveal the name(s) of the victim(s) or the location, date, or time of any crimes.

8. **Fraud & Hot Checks**: Have you ever engaged in or attempted to engage in fraud? Include in this item fraud, forgery, hot checks, impersonating someone, use of another person's credit card, con games, and/or scams or schemes to cheat others out of money. <u>Fifth Amendment Right</u> – Do not reveal the name(s) of the victim(s) or the location, date, or time of any crimes.

9. **Escape & Absconding**: Have you ever attempted to escape or actually escaped from law enforcement? Include in this item escape from lawful custody; breaking out of jail, detention, or state school; failure to appear at a scheduled court hearing; jumping bail; and/or violation of probation, parole, or bond. <u>Fifth Amendment Right</u> – Do not reveal the name(s) of the victim(s) or the location, date, or time of any crimes.

10. **Kidnapping**: Have you ever attempted or engaged in kidnapping? Include kidnapping, abduction, hijacking, carjacking, and/or unlawful confinement of another. <u>Fifth Amendment Right</u> – Do not reveal the name(s) of the victim(s) or the location, date, or time of any crimes.

11. **Arson**: Have you ever attempted or engaged in arson? <u>Fifth Amendment Right</u> – Do not reveal the name(s) of the victim(s) or the location, date, or time of any crimes.

12. **Obstruction of Justice & False ID**: Have you ever attempted or engaged in obstruction of justice? Include in this item perjury, assault of a police officer, lying to a police officer, resisting arrest, and/or contempt of court. Fifth Amendment Right – Do not reveal the name(s) of the victim(s) or the location, date, or time of any crimes.

13. **Misdemeanor:** Have you ever attempted or engaged in misdemeanor crimes? Include in this item vandalism, trespassing, disorderly conduct, criminal mischief, criminal damage, driving without a license, and/or bookmaking. Fifth Amendment Right – Do not reveal the name(s) of the victim(s) or the location, date, or time of any crimes.

14. **Miscellaneous:** Have you ever attempted or engaged in any other crimes that are not covered in the other items? If so, write down those crimes. Remember, you want to be honest and reveal as much as possible, so you can leave the "old me" in the past. Fifth Amendment Right – Do not reveal the name(s) of the victim(s) or the location, date, or time of any crimes.

What I Learned about Myself from My Criminal History

In this assignment, you will be asked to write about what you learned about yourself while completing your Criminal History Assignment. In order to do this assignment correctly you must have already completed your Criminal History Questionnaire. The purpose of this assignment is for you to learn from your past.

1. **<u>Describe the criminal behavior that you have engaged in throughout your lifetime.</u>**

   When were the first and last times you used this criminal behavior? What types of criminal behavior have you used and how many times have you used each type of behavior? Do you show a preference for a particular type of behavior? How has your use of criminal behavior changed over your lifetime?

2. **<u>Describe how your criminal life has affected your loved ones.</u>**

   How has your criminal behavior affected those you love? What price have your loved ones paid because of your criminal conduct? How has your criminal behavior affected the way that your family and friends think of you? What kind of effect has your criminal behavior had on your relationships?

3. **<u>Explain how you have suffered as a result of your criminal conduct.</u>**

   In what ways have you suffered because of your criminal history? What have you lost because of your criminal history? Losses can include things like lost time and freedom because you were locked up, lost relationships, lost income, lost opportunities, loss of respect, and so on.

4. **<u>Are you changing?</u>**

   Have you started to change from a criminal lifestyle to a citizen lifestyle? If so, explain how you have changed. How have your thinking, emotions, and relationships changed?

5. **<u>What kind of future will you have?</u>**

   If you keep up your pattern of criminal behavior, what kind of future will you have? If you make the switch to a citizen lifestyle, what kind of future will you have? Which do you choose, a criminal or citizen lifestyle? Why did you make that choice?

Module Three: Self-Control

Crimes do not just happen. Before someone commits a crime, he or she has to want to commit the crime, come up with a plan, and then set up the situation so the crime can be committed. All of these things happen before the crime. That is why we say, *"Crimes do not just happen."*

Law enforcement knows that crimes don't just happen. When law enforcement officials talk about this subject, they refer to it as someone's modus operandi, or MO. According to law enforcement, a person's MO is comprised of two parts.

First, the MO is anything that the person does to make sure he or she can commit the crime and escape. Second, not all crimes are committed the same way and the personal touch that a criminal puts on a crime is known as his or her "signature." For example, one criminal who burglarizes homes breaks into the homes by throwing patio furniture through the back door. Another criminal might just kick in the front door. Each of these criminals had to break into the house to burglarize it, but each one had a signature way of breaking in.

Treatment experts have borrowed the concept of MO from law enforcement and converted it to something called "stair steps." Just like the MO captures an individual's personal way of committing crimes, the stair steps are an individual's pattern of committing a particular type of crime. In treatment, you are expected to be able to identify your criminal pattern, or stair steps, and then develop ways of getting off the stair steps, so you have **No More Victims**! The stair steps are all about changing from the "old me" to the "new me."

There is a Cherokee fable that might help you create a picture in your mind about what it is like to change from "old me" to "new me." In this fable, a grandfather is helping his teenage grandson deal with a personal struggle very much like the struggle you are dealing with. The wise words the grandfather shared with his grandson might just apply to you.

A teenage warrior goes to his grandfather's tepee to discuss a problem. The young warrior says, "There is a terrible fight going on inside me. It is like I have two wolves inside me and they are fighting. One wolf is evil, and it wants me to do evil things. When the evil wolf is stronger, I do not do the right things. I do bad things and I hurt others. The other wolf is good, and it wants me to do good things. When the good wolf is strong, I do good things. I feel strong and powerful. I am closer to my family and my tribe. These two wolves are constantly at each other's necks. They give me no peace. Grandfather, I don't know what to do and I am afraid. Tell me, which wolf will win? I must know!"

The grandfather put his hand on the shoulder of the young warrior and simply said, "That is easy. The wolf that you feed will win."

What are the Stair Steps?

Think of the steps you took leading up to your crime as steps on stairs. Each step is a thought, feeling, or action you took. Each step you took brought you closer to committing a crime.

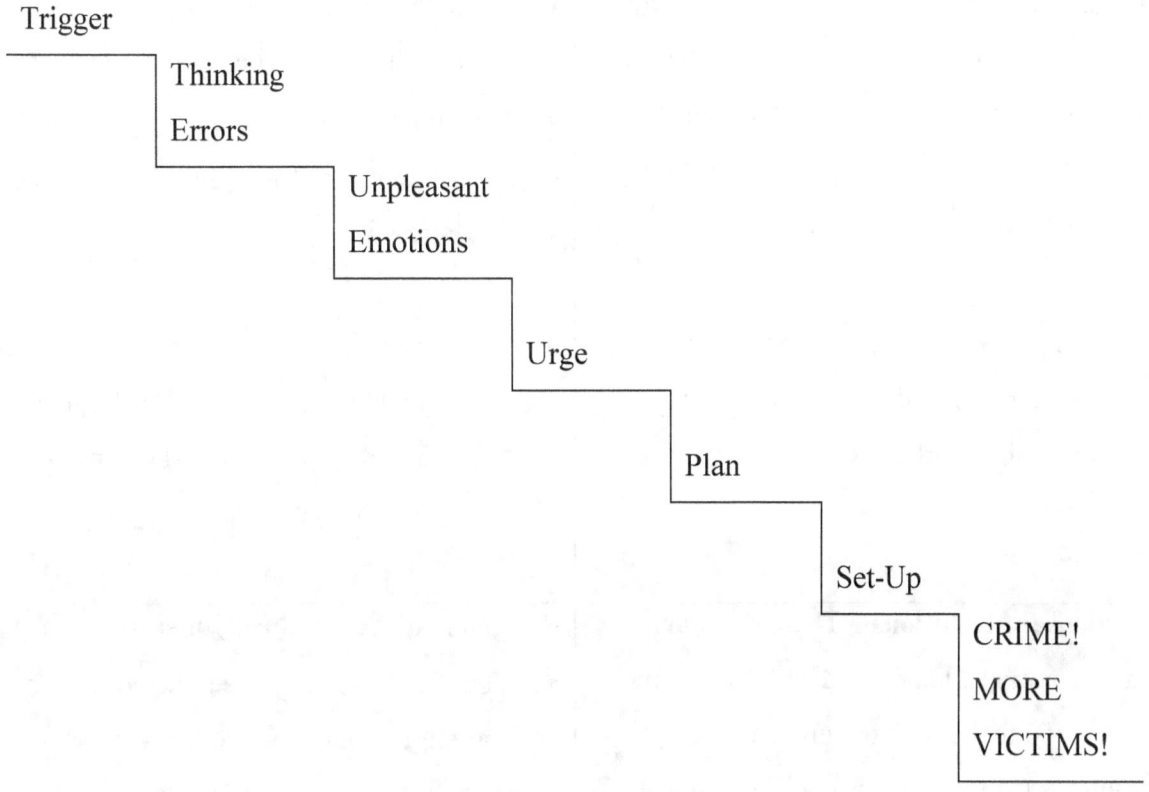

You do not get on the stair steps until you have a trigger (stress in your life). After the trigger happens, you begin to think about it. You use thinking errors when you think about the trigger. The thinking errors don't make you feel better; they make you feel an unpleasant emotion. They make you feel sad, mad, or scared.

Like any other person, when you feel an unpleasant emotion, you want to feel better. You start to imagine things that might make you feel better. You get urges, and some of those urges are criminal urges.

Once you decide to give in to your criminal urges, you start planning your offense. Next, you set up your victim. Finally, you commit the offense. That is how you walk down the stair steps and commit an offense.

Stair Steps	Signs That You Are on This Step of the Stair Steps
Trigger – Any stress can be a trigger. Most triggers are conflicts with important people in your life. Doing drugs is not a trigger. You've already committed a crime if you are doing drugs.	• Arguing with boyfriend or girlfriend, family, friends, teachers, employers, etc. • No money • Restrictions because of probation or parole • Any stress in your life
Thinking Errors – You use one of the thinking errors listed in the orientation section of this workbook.	• Common thinking errors about the trigger often include "power play," "selfishness," "entitlement," "poor me," "keeping score," and "Mr. Goodguy/Ms. Goodgal."
Unpleasant Emotions – There are four basic emotions: happy, sad, scared, and mad. When you feel one of the unpleasant emotions (sad, scared, or mad), you try to escape the unpleasant feeling via criminal urges.	• You may feel sad, mad, or scared. • You may not recognize the emotions, but you might notice that your body has changed: increased heart rate, increased breathing rate, clenched fists, pacing, etc.
Urge –-An urge is the mental picture in your mind of committing the offense. Every mental image creates a feeling. The feeling that you get when you think about the behavior is usually a pleasant, happy emotion. The criminal urge is the first step	• You spend time picturing what it would be like to commit the offense. • You imagine how much better the offense will make you feel.

of a behavior you use to escape the unpleasant feelings caused by the trigger.	• You daydream about how much better your life will be once you have committed the offense.
Plan – Planning is figuring out the best way to commit the offense and escape. Some plans are simple; others are complicated. When you plan, you get many ideas about when, where, and how to commit the offense. You may find that planning the offense makes you feel happy and excited.	• You consider different times and places to commit the offense. • You try to pick the perfect victim. • You recall past successes and try to figure out how to do it again.
Set-Up – A set-up is anything that you do to isolate the victim so you can exploit him or her. Anything that you do to keep family and friends from knowing about your criminal urges, plans, and acts is also part of the set-up.	• You watch the victim and try to find his or her weaknesses • You watch the victim and try to find the best time to commit the crime. • You put up a false front around family, friends, and other citizens.

Assignment

1. Get a notebook. Write down each step of the stair steps. Leave plenty of room between each step. You will be describing each step in detail.

2. Focus on one criminal offense you committed. Make it an important offense, like the instant offense that got you into this program.

3. Break down the offense you selected and show how you completed each step of the stair steps. Start at the bottom of the stair steps and work backwards. For example, write down the crime. Then write down how you set-up the crime an keep working backwards until you get to the trigger.

4. Present the assignment in a group session and revise the assignment based on the feedback you get. Keep revising until your treatment provider approves the assignment.

Coping with Triggers

A trigger is anything that is stressful. Life is stressful. You can never escape stress, so you will always have triggers.

Since you cannot eliminate triggers, how you cope with triggers is very important. You have a choice about how you cope with triggers. In fact, there are two ways to cope with triggers:

- **Harmful** – Your "old me" used to deal with stress by breaking rules or committing an offense. This does not relieve stress – it can actually create more stress. Here is how your "old me" could create more stress: stress could start out as one problem; for example, you could have an argument with your mother. If you deal with the stress by committing a crime, you have created another problem. You still have the original problem, but your response to the problem has created another problem. How smart is that? Now you have two problems instead of one.
- **Healthy** – The healthy person, the "new me," deals with stress by following rules. The healthy person tries to deal with the problem directly, using the guidelines approved by society. The healthy person does not create more problems. Even if it takes the healthy person a long time to solve the problem, the healthy person still just has one problem.

You must understand that triggers do not make you commit a crime. You make choices. You always have two choices: you can choose to act like the "old me" and commit a crime, or you can choose to act like the "new me" and follow rules.

You will always have stress in your life, so you will always have a choice to make. The choice is simple: do you want to be the "old me" or do you want to be the "new me"? One path leads to your destruction and the other to happiness and success. Choose wisely.

Assignment

1. What is a trigger?

2. What are the two ways of coping with a trigger?

3. Do triggers make you commit crimes?

4. Will you ever be free from triggers in your life?

5. What was your trigger when you committed your instant offense?

6. What kind of stress do you have in your life right now?

7. Could the stress in your life right now be a trigger? Explain your answer.

8. How are dealing with the stress that you have in your life right now – like the "old me" or the "new me"?

Coping with Thinking Errors

When you used the Thought Journal, you learned how to recognize and label thinking errors. It is not enough to recognize and label a thinking error, though – you must learn how to quit using thinking errors. The Triple Column Technique is the best way to learn how to eliminate thinking errors.

The Triple Column Technique is very similar to the Thought Journal. When you use the Triple Column Technique, you must identify your thoughts and label your thinking errors, just as you did when you wrote your Thought Journal. However, there is one extra step to the Triple Column Technique. Once you have identified your thinking error, you must have a debate with yourself. You must talk yourself out of the thinking error. In this way, you can learn to defeat your own thinking errors.

Directions:

1. Get a piece of paper. Draw two lines down the length of the paper, i.e. vertical lines, creating three columns on the paper.

2. Label the first column "Thought." The next two columns are labeled "Thinking Error(s)" and "Solution."

3. In the first column, make entries of thoughts that you had during the day. The entries should be only your thoughts. Do not list activities or emotions.

4. Next, analyze the thought that you wrote and identify any thinking errors that you can find. List thinking errors in the middle column.

5. In the third column, talk yourself out of the thought and the thinking error by explaining to yourself why you should not think this way and why you should not use the thinking error(s) that you identified. The solution must be more believable to you than the original thought – otherwise you will continue to believe the thinking error. It is better to write nothing in the third column than something that you do not believe.

6. Turn in this assignment weekly, until your treatment provider instructs you to stop doing the assignment.

Samples of the Triple Column Technique

Thought	Thinking Error(s)	Solution
My neighbor yelled at me for walking across his lawn. "F" him. I will walk wherever I want. He can't tell me what to do.	Keeping Score Power Play Entitlement	*It is his lawn, and there is a perfectly good sidewalk nearby. I don't need to be stirring up problems in the neighborhood. What happens if my probation officer talks with the neighbors?*

Thought	Thinking Error(s)	Solution
I have had such a rough day. I need to hit a blunt. I will only do one hit. No one will know.	Poor Me Minimizing Super Optimism	*Get real. I get drug tested all the time. They will know. I think they are just looking for a way to send me back. I don't want to give them any ammunition they can use to hurt me.*

Thought	Thinking Error(s)	Solution
My girlfriend just dumped me – unreal! What a "B"! What did I do? I am a good guy. She just doesn't understand me.	Poor me Anger Keeping Score Mr. Goodguy	*I know why she dumped me. I was talking with her cousin and her cousin told her. I wasn't loyal. I have no one to blame but myself. That is what players get –they get dumped.*

Coping with Emotions

There are four basic emotions: happiness, sadness, anger, and fear. Happiness is a pleasant emotion. The three unpleasant emotions are sadness, anger, and fear.

Even though some emotions are unpleasant, all emotions are good because all emotions can give you important information – even unpleasant emotions. Don't believe me? Consider this: let's say you are about to do something really stupid, but you are feeling some worry or fear. Should listen to your fear? Your fear is telling you that if you do this thing, you will be hurt. If you don't want go get hurt, you listen to your fear. If you don't listen to your fear, chances are you get hurt. Even unpleasant emotions can be good, if you are willing to listen to them.

Before you committed your offense, your emotions were probably trying to tell you not to commit the crime. You didn't listen…but that was your "old me." Your "old me" didn't know how to deal with emotions. Now you are trying to change your ways and become the type of person who can deal with emotions, even unpleasant emotions.

There are two basic ways to deal with unpleasant emotions – unhealthy and healthy. You always have a choice about how you deal with your emotions:

- **Old Me** – Your "old me" made two mistakes when dealing with unpleasant emotions. First, you wanted rapid relief from the unpleasant emotion, so you chose to commit crimes to get relief from the unpleasant emotions. Second, your "old me" couldn't control the unpleasant emotions, and you let your emotions spill over onto other people. It's like the old saying, "Misery Loves Company." When the "old you" felt an unpleasant emotion, you tried to make others feel unpleasant emotions.

- **New Me** – The main way that a healthy person deals with unpleasant emotions is by talking about those feelings. By talking about the unpleasant emotions, the healthy person does not have to keep the emotions inside. The other person can help by sharing the burden of the unpleasant emotions. Talking is the way that your "new me" should be coping with unpleasant emotions.

When you talk about emotions, you need to talk about the roots of the emotions, or what caused each emotion. Different emotions have different roots:

- **Anger** – You can't feel anger without first being hurt. Hurt is the root of anger. When you feel anger, talk about the hurt. Do not talk about how angry you are.
- **Sadness** – Sadness is a sign that you lost something. Loss is the root of sadness. When you feel sadness, talk about your loss.
- **Fear** – The root of fear is a threat. You can only feel fear when there is a threat. Some threats are real. Some threats are not real; they are just in your mind. When you feel fear, talk about the threat.

If you want to talk about your emotions, be careful. Sometimes talking about your emotions can get you pumped up, and you can become angrier. If you find yourself getting pumped up, you are definitely not talking about your emotions in the correct way. Remember, you must talk about the roots of the emotions.

You had unpleasant emotions in the past, and you will have them in the future. Now that you know how emotions work, you have a choice. You can do things the way your "old me" did them and create more problems for yourself – or you can try being a "new me" and coping with emotions like a healthy person does, by talking about the roots of the emotions. There are two paths – "old me" and "new me." The choice is yours.

Assignment

1. What are the three unpleasant emotions?
2. How can unpleasant emotions lead to an offense?
3. What is the root of anger?
4. What is the root of sadness?
5. What is the root of fear?
6. What is the harmful way of coping with emotions?
7. What is the healthy way of coping with emotions?

Coping with Urges

Urges are automatic, and sometimes you just can't stop them from popping into your mind. Even if you can't stop an urge from popping into your mind, you can choose what do with your urge. You can choose to control your urge or to give into your urge and commit a crime. You always have a choice when it comes to urges.

If you want to become good at controlling your urges, you should use the Urge Log. The Urge Log is simply a way of keeping track of the urges you get and how you respond to those urges. You can use the Urge Log to learn how to become more effective at dealing with urges. That is the power of the Urge Log. You can learn to recognize and control your urges. This is an important part of making the shift from "old me" to "new me."

Directions:

1. Obtain some notebook paper to use as your Urge Log. Use only the front sides of the pages; do not write on the backs of the pages. Print or use legible handwriting. If your handwriting is not legible, you may be required to type your journal.

2. Make four columns on the page. Label each column:
    A) **Event** – Give the day, time, place, and people involved in the event.
    B) **Urge** – Describe your urge, i.e., what did you want to do in response to the event? Many times, the urge you get will be for a criminal outlet.
    C) **Rating of Intensity** – On a scale of one to ten, with ten being the strongest, rate how strong your urge was.
    D) **Control Technique** – Describe how you controlled your urge. You may want to refer to the self-control techniques in this treatment manual.

3. Carry your log with you at all times. When you experience an urge, complete an entry in your log.

4. Turn your log in to your treatment provider every week.

5. Complete a new log every week while in this stage, or until your treatment provider tells you that you can stop doing this assignment.

Coping with Set-Ups

A set-up is anything that you do to commit an offense and get away with it. There are two parts to a set-up. First is the part where you set up the situation so you can commit a crime. Second is the part where you make sure that you can escape.

Set Up the Situation – When you commit an offense, you have to set up the victim and anybody who you think might want to stop you. If your crime was against a person, you had to set up the person you victimized and anyone who could have stopped you from hurting that person. If your crime was a property or drug crime, you set up the situation by controlling or manipulating anyone who could have stopped you from committing the offense.

Escape – You did not want to get caught for committing your crime, so you did what you thought would keep others from catching you. You might have done something simple, like keeping a secret. At other times, you might have had to do a lot more than just keep secrets. You might have had to lie, manipulate, or distract to make sure you could get away with your crime.

You spent a lot of time trying to figure out the best way to set up your crime, and you still got caught. If you can't believe you got caught, you need to re-read the introduction section of this workbook. You will realize that it is only a matter of time before anyone is caught for his or her crime, no matter how good the set-up was.

You need to know that you also set up yourself. You made yourself think that there was a right way of committing your offense. You did not pay attention to the thing that healthy people know: **there is no right way to do a wrong thing.**

Assignment

1. Is there any right way to do a set-up?
2. How did you set up the victim(s) of your offense?
3. How did you set up yourself?

My Plan for Getting off the Stair Steps

Any stress can be a trigger for you, and that can cause you to be on the stair steps. Once you are on the stair steps, you have a choice. Your "old me" would go all the way down the stair steps until you reached the bottom and hurt yourself and somebody else.

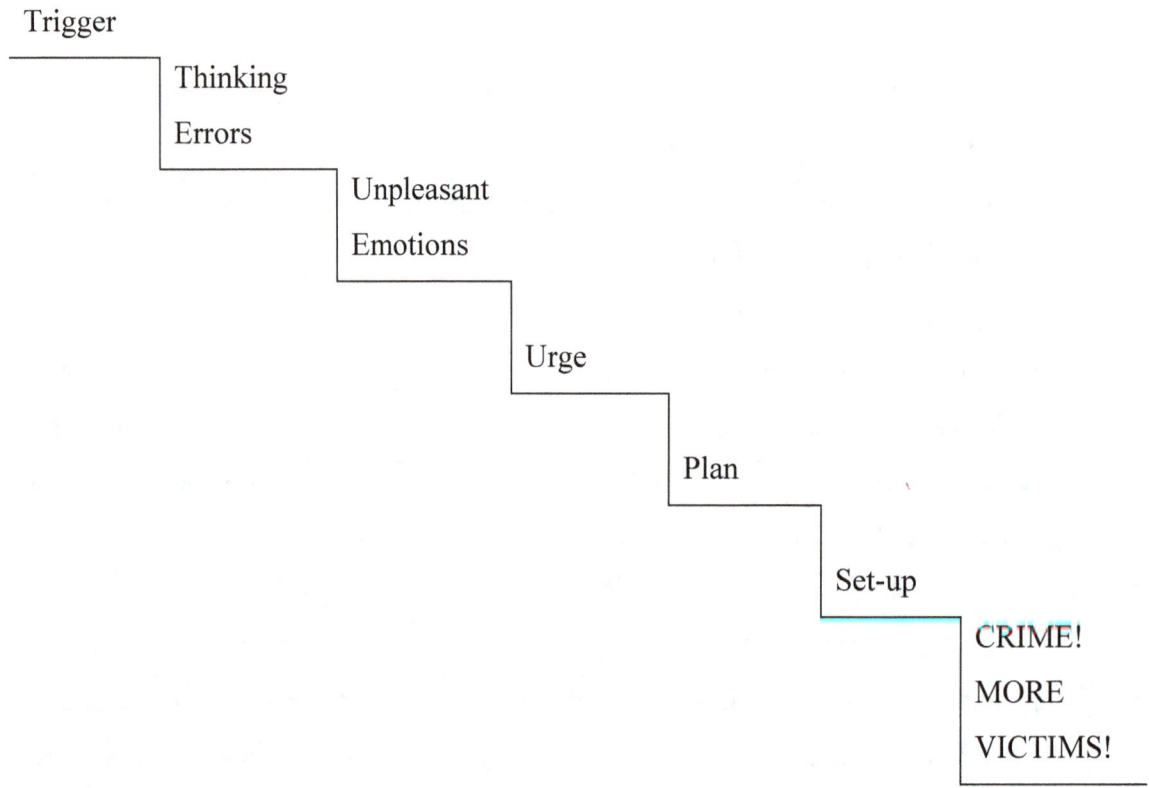

Trigger

Thinking Errors

Unpleasant Emotions

Urge

Plan

Set-up

CRIME! MORE VICTIMS!

It doesn't have to be that way; you don't have to let your "old me" mess everything up. Your "new me" can jump off the stair steps before you get to the bottom. Do you know how to jump off your stair steps? Easy – for each of the stair steps, figure out a way to cope with that step like a citizen. Citizens don't create victims. If you behave like a citizen, you will have **No More Victims!**

Assignment

1. Figure out how to get off the stair steps by focusing on one of the crimes you committed. First, think of <u>one</u> crime you committed. List that crime at the bottom of the stair steps. Then write down how you set-up the crime. Keep working backwards up the stair steps until you list the trigger.

2. Now work back down the stair steps starting with the trigger. Write a plan for how you could cope with that trigger if that trigger happened again in your life. Go to the next step and write about how you would cope with the thinking errors if those same thinking errors happened in your life today. Keep working down the stair steps until you have written a plan for how you will cope with each step of the stair steps.

    Please be aware that even if you go all the way down the stair steps and commit a another crime, you still have to come up with a way of coping with that step of the stair steps. In other words, you have come up with a way of making sure one crime doesn't turn into many crimes. Committing one crime doesn't mean you have to return to a life of crime. The "new me" can cope with a new crime, which can prevent your "old me" from taking over and ruining your life.

Module Four: Your Support Group

You should begin work on Module Four as soon as you begin this treatment program. This module is designed to get your loved ones involved in helping you create the "new me." The family and friends that you enlist to help you with treatment are called your support group. You will take three steps when building your support group:

1. Identify the people you want to be in your support group.
2. Ask each of these people to be in your support group.
3. Create a Support Group Contract between you and the people in your support group.

These steps sound easy, but they are not. These steps might be the most important steps that you take on the journey from "old me" to "new me." You will have to overcome a great deal of self-doubt. You will have to risk being open and honest. In the end, though, your efforts will be rewarded. The important people in your life will know about your problem with crime. They will be trained to support you as you work on your problem, and they will become your lifelong support group.

Help from Daniel

Daniel was a client in a treatment program very much like the one you are in. Just like you, one of the things he had to do was to create a support group. Just like you, Daniel had to struggle with secrecy and honesty. Here is what he had to say:

If you are reading this, then like me, your behavior has gotten you into trouble. Actually, secrecy is probably what got me into trouble. Secrecy is something that you must part with if you wish to be a success. You probably have someone who cares about you.

Chances are that this person has only part of the facts about your crime and victims. Whoever you chose to be a part of your treatment, you are going to have to be honest. You cannot keep secrets.

The people you get involved in your treatment probably know your victim and your crime. As often is the case in these circumstances, there are probably some things that these people don't know about your crime. It is <u>NECESSARY</u> that you reveal everything and put your relationship back on honest ground.

There is always a chance that your honesty might end a relationship. Don't take a chance on ending your relationships. Don't be brutally honest all at once. It can shock people. Let the important people in your life become a part of treatment. The treatment staff can help you decide when to how much to reveal at a time.

Inform the people that you care about that you need to be honest to succeed. Tell them that you need to be able to trust them with the truth. Reveal your secrets, and by doing so you can remain in and progress through group sessions and treatment. GOOD LUCK!

I Need the Help of Those Who Love Me

Your "old me" is the person who committed crimes. You are trying to create a "new me," a person who will be happy and successful and who will have **No More Victims!**

When the "old me" was in charge, you kept secrets from those who loved you. You isolated yourself. You kept your loved ones at a distance. All that needs to change. Secrets were the foundation for the "old me." Secrets are the foundation for a new offense and more victims. Now that you are in this treatment program, your goal is **No More Victims!** You need to eliminate secrets from your life if you are to reach that goal.

You need to be open and honest about your "old me" with those who love you. This is the only way that you can get the help that you need.

You have probably told yourself a lot of things to justify keeping secrets from your loved ones. Have you told yourself any of the following things?

- If I tell them about my crimes, they won't love me or care for me.
- It is too embarrassing to talk about the "old me" and all the things I used to do.
- I want to protect them from having to hear bad things about me.
- I fear that my relationship with my loved ones might change if I tell them.

No matter what you have been telling yourself to justify keeping secrets, you are wrong. You need the help of your loved ones, and you can only get their help if you are open and honest. Secrecy is an "old me" attitude. Honesty is the cure for secrecy. Honesty is the attitude of the "new me."

The purpose for being honest is not to make you feel guilt or shame. There are two goals you will meet when you are honest with others:

Monitoring – When you are honest with your loved ones about your "old me," they can monitor you and give you feedback if they see that you are slipping back into the "old me" way of behaving. Your loved ones can also give your treatment provider feedback about your behavior. Based on this feedback, your treatment provider can change your treatment to increase your chances of being a success.

Healthy Relationships – When you are honest with your loved ones about your past, you are increasing your honesty. Honesty is the basis of healthy relationships. When you are honest, you are building a solid foundation. You have a much better chance of being happy and successful.

Being honest with your loved ones is an important part of changing from "old me" to "new me." Of course, you will be frightened about being honest. You will be tempted to keep your "old me" a secret.

You must remember that secrecy is the thing that keeps your "old me" alive. Honesty can break your "old me" and give you the chance for true happiness and freedom. Once your secrets are eliminated, you can relate to others in a healthy way. This is an important step towards **No More Victims.**

Assignment

1. What secrets did you keep from your loved ones about your "old me"?
2. Which loved ones have you told about your "old me"? Have you been honest?
3. What secrets do you continue to keep about your "old me"?
4. What do you tell yourself that makes it okay to keep secrets from your loved ones?
5. How are you going to increase your honesty with your loved ones?

The People in My Support Group

Anyone who loves you and wants you to be a citizen can be in your support group. Your support group can include people like your boyfriend or girlfriend, parents, relatives, or good friends. It does not matter who your source of support is, so long as they love you and they want you to be a citizen.

You probably know which people in your life really love you, but do you know which people in your life want you to be a citizen? There are two types of things that your loved ones can do help you become a citizen, so consider which of your loved ones would be willing to help you in the following ways:

- **During Treatment** – During treatment, your loved ones can help you become a citizen by encouraging you and helping you complete assignments in this workbook. Your loved ones can also help you become a citizen by talking with your treatment provider and other staff and letting them know how you are doing.

- **After Treatment** – After treatment is over, you will no longer have contact with your treatment provider or other staff, but you will still need support. The loved ones who are willing to help you form your citizen lifestyle are those who will support you when you try to maintain your citizen lifestyle, and they will confront you if they see that you are backsliding. They will replace your treatment provider and be a source of positive influence for the rest of your life.

The people you select to be part of your support group must be good role models and must have a good influence on you. If you hang around people who do bad things, your "old me" will gain strength and you will slip back into your "old me" ways. If you hang around people who are citizens, it will be easier for your "new me" to grow strong, and you will become happy and successful.

Assignment

1. Name the loved ones who you want to be part of your support group.

2. For each person listed, respond to the following questions:

    A. What is this person's relationship with you?

    B. How often do you have contact with this person?

    C. Can this person attend therapy sessions with you?

    D. Is this person a positive influence? Does this person know about the "old me"? Is the person strong enough to love you and still admit that you did something wrong? Does this person make excuses for you or minimize your offense?

3. Who will be part of your support group?

Letter to My Support Group

Now that you have chosen the people who you want to be in your support group, you need to ask them to be members of your support group. It can be difficult to ask for help. It is especially difficult to ask for help with the "old me." You can write a letter, and when you meet with your support group, you can read the letter to them. That will make it much easier to ask for the help you need.

Assignment

1. Write a letter to the people in your support group. One letter may be written for everyone in your support group; it is not necessary to write a separate letter for each person. In the letter, you must tell these persons about the "old me" and what they could do to help you be the "new me." You will read the letter to them with the help of your treatment provider.

2. When you write the letter to your support group, use the outline below:

   A. **Greeting** – Let them know that you are in treatment and that if you are going to be a success, you will need the help of important people in your life. Let them know they are the important people who can help you.

   B. **Self-Disclosure** – Tell them about the "old me." Do not blame or minimize. You can use information from the Offense Summary Worksheet, Criminal History Worksheet, and other assignments in this workbook to describe the "old me."

   C. **Goal** – Let the person know the goal of treatment is **No More Victims**! Explain the goal. Explain why it is important to you.

   D. **Request for Help** – Explain how the members of your support group can help you reach the goal of **No More Victims**! Remember that they can help you while you are in treatment and after treatment is over. Explain the ways that your loved ones can help you now and in the future.

   E. **Conclusion** – Let the members of your support group know that you would appreciate their help, but that it is up to them if they want to help. Let them know that your treatment provider will be available to answer questions.

3. Read the letter during a group or individual therapy session before you share it with your support group. Accept feedback that is given to you. Revise and present the letter again in therapy sessions, until you don't get any more feedback.

4. Set an appointment time with your treatment provider to meet with the persons in your support group.

5. Sign a Release of Confidential Information allowing your treatment provider to communicate with persons in your support group.

6. Meet with the persons in your support group and read the letter. Make sure that your treatment provider and all the persons in your support group attend the meeting.

Contract with My Support Group

Now that you have a support group, you need to provide them with specific details about how they can help you. The easiest way for you to let them know how to help you is to develop a Support Group Contract. This is a contract between you and the members of your support group about what you must do to and how they can help you.

The thing you are trying to do is to transition from "old me" to "new me." You have to describe all the things you are doing to create the "new me" so your support group can help you.

It is not enough for you tell others about how you are trying to change. You also have to tell them how they can help you change.

Use the following outline to create your Support Group Contract. Carefully read and answer each item, so you can write the best possible Support Group Contract.

1. **Monitoring** – Your support group needs to help you watch for signs that your "old me" is making a comeback. Your "old me" is making a comeback when you start putting yourself in high-risk situations. Remember, a high-risk situation can be a person, place or thing. Your "old me" is making a comeback when you put yourself in contact with persons, places or things that make it easier for you to use criminal outlets. **Assignment:** List some signs that your "old me" is making a comeback. List three high-risk persons, three high-risk places, and three high-risk things that show you are backsliding.

2. **Feedback** – Let your loved ones know the best way they can give you feedback when they see signs of the "old you." **Assignment:** Write down specific things your support group can say to help get you back on track. Also write down how you will respond to their feedback.

3. **Recognizing the "New Me"** – Your support group needs to know the ways in which you are changing, so they can support the changes you have made. In other words, your support group needs to know the "new me" so they can help you become the "new me" you want to be. **Assignment**: The "new me" is going to show up in the ways you think and feel. It will also show up in the ways you interact with others. Describe the "new me"

by describing the new ways the "new me" thinks, feels, and relates to others. You should be able to list at least three new ways you think, three new ways you feel or express emotions, and three new ways you relate to others.

4. **Support and Praise** – There are two ways that your support group can help you become the "new me" you want to be. First they can support you or help you as you try to create a new lifestyle. Second, they can praise you when they find you doing something right. **Assignment:** List three things that your support group can do to support you as you transition to your "new me." List three ways your support group can praise you for positive behavior.

5. **Signatures and Approval** – At the end of your Support Group Contract, you need to make some spaces for you and your support group members to sign the contract. You should also create spaces for your treatment provider and supervising officer to sign the contract.

Above the space where you will sign, you need to write the following statement of agreement: "I agree to abide by the rules and agreements written in this contract." Leave a space for your signature.

Above the space where your support group will sign, you need to write the following statement of agreement: "I agree to abide by the rules and agreements in this contract. I agree to attend therapy sessions with my loved one when I can. I agree to report to the treatment provider when my loved one does not follow the contract." Leave spaces for the members of your support group to sign.

Watch Out for Splitting

Splitting is anything that you do to split your support group and your treatment provider. A good image for splitting is the image of splitting wood. When you split wood, you drive a wedge into a log. The log is split and you have two pieces instead of one solid log.

When you get your support group to keep a secret from your treatment provider, you have split your support group and your treatment provider. Other clients who have split their treatment provider and support group usually ask – or force – a member of their support group to keep secrets about violations of the Support Group Contract.

If you are going to get the most out of your Support Group Contract, you need your treatment provider and your support group to work together. The more help you have, the better chance you have of being a success.

If you even think about trying to get someone in your support group to keep a secret, you have started a split. The only way to prevent a split is to not keep secrets. The only way to stop a split once it has started it is to reveal your secret.

Assignment

1. What is splitting?
2. How do secrets create splitting?
3. For each person in your support group, list at least three ways you might try to split them from your treatment provider.
4. Show your splitting list to the members of your support group. Together, you and the members of your support group should come up with a specific way to defeat each of the ways you might try to create a split.

Support Group Problem Solving

You know that there can be problems in any relationship. There is no question of *if* a relationship will have problems; it is a question of *when* the relationship will have problems. The problems that you might have with your support group could include:

1. **Resentment** – You might resent that your support group is monitoring your behavior and watching for signs of the "old me."

2. **Closed Channel** – You might want to keep some things to yourself and not share them with the members of your support group.

3. **Power Play** – You might get into a power struggle with one or more of the members of your support group.

If you can have problems with your support group, it should not surprise you to learn that the members of your support group can also have problems with you:

1. **Resentment** – Someone in your support group might resent having to constantly monitor you and watch for signs that your "old me" is making a comeback.

2. **Closed Channel** – Someone in your support group may want to talk to you about certain things but decide to keep things bottled up.

3. **Power Play** – Someone in your support group might get frustrated with all the rules and requirements of the Support Group Contract and try to get you not to follow them.

It is true that every relationship has problems. It is also true that a relationship does not have to end just because there are problems. Relationships survive and thrive because the people in them can work through problems.

You have learned a way to solve problems that also works for relationship problems. You already know how to use the Why Sandwich. When you start to experience problems in your relationship with your support group, you can use the Why Sandwich.

What: What is the Problem?

If you and someone in your support group are having problems, describe the problem by answering the questions listed below.

What is the problem?	*Where did it happen?*
Who is involved?	*How many times has it happened?*
When did it happen?	*How did it start?*
How did it happen?	*Who knows about the problem?*

Why: Why is it a problem?

It is not enough to be able to describe the problem; you have to be able to explain why the problem is important. Your responses to the following questions should tell you why it is important.

Why is it a problem?	*Why do others think it is a problem?*
Are other people hurt?	*Is it part of a cycle?*
Why is it a problem for me?	*Why is it a problem for other people?*

What: What am I going to do about the problem?

Once you have identified your problem and you understand why it is problem, you need to do something about it. Ask yourself the following questions so you can come up with a plan of action for eliminating your problem. Remember to take action once you have a plan.

What can I do?	*How can I prevent the problem in the future?*
Can anyone help me?	*What have other people done in a similar situation?*

You and the members of your support group need to learn how to use the Why Sandwich to solve problems with the Support Group Contract. If you get good at using the Why Sandwich with your support group, you will improve your relationship with the members of your support group. You will probably also improve your relationship with just about everybody else you interact with.

Assignment

1. Pick someone in your support group to do this assignment with. You can pick two people if you want, e.g., your mother and father.

2. Come up with a list of problems that you have with the person you picked do this assignment with. Ask the person from your support group to make a list of problems he or she has with you.

3. Meet with the member of the support group. Pick one problem from the list you and your support group member created. Use the Why Sandwich to solve this problem.

4. Once you have found a solution to the problem, describe how you will monitor the solution. Set a time to review progress towards solving the problem.

5. Participate in a review meeting with your support group member for the purpose of seeing if the solution from the Why Sandwich is working. If the solution is not working, use the Why Sandwich again and come up with a new solution.

6. Keep monitoring and revising your solution until you and your support group member solve the problem. Remember that you can always ask your treatment provider for help at any stage in the problem solving process.

Module Five: Preparing for a Citizen Lifestyle

A scientist conducted an experiment on coping skills. The subjects in the experiment were two frogs. Each frog experienced a different condition, and the way the frogs responded teach us a lot about coping skills.

- **Condition One** – The frog was put in a pot of water on a stove. When the frog got into the water, it was a good temperature for the frog. The experimenter turned the heat up on the frog but he did this slowly, about one degree every 10 minutes or so. Eventually, the water became so hot that the frog died from the heat. The frog never jumped out because the change was so slow and gradual that the frog never noticed the change.

- **Condition Two** – The experimenter took another frog and put it into a pot of water that was the exact temperature that killed the frog in Condition One. When the second frog was put into the pot, the second frog jumped and jumped until he got out of the pot of water. This frog went from a condition of being comfortable to a condition of being in shock and needing to cope.

After years and years of watching clients try to change from an "old me" to a "new me," it is clear that most clients can make significant change. It is also clear that it is very difficult to hold onto positive changes. The reason is simple: old habits from the "old me" creep in very slowly, in small steps. The change back to your "old me" is so gradual that you don't notice it. Then one day you look up and you say, *"Oh, no! How did this happen? How did I start acting this way again?"*

The answer to those questions is very easy. The change back to the "old me" happened so gradually you never noticed it. You never knew you needed to cope, so you did nothing to stop the comeback of your "old me." You were like the frog in Condition One. You didn't cope because you didn't know that you needed to cope.

If you want to notice when old habits are creeping back into your life, you have to notice the slow process of relapse and stop yourself. When you see that you are relapsing, you must choose to return to healthy behavior instead of slowly slipping back into bad habits. The goal of this part of the workbook is for you to develop your own personal method of seeing when old habits are creeping back in, so you can use the skills that you developed during treatment.

If you want to appreciate how important habits are, just consider the things some great people have said about habits throughout the history of civilization:

- *"It is easier to prevent bad habits than break them."* –Ben Franklin
- *"We first make our habits, then our habits make us."* –John Dryden
- *"Winning is a habit. Unfortunately, so is losing."* –Vince Lombardi
- *"We are what we repeatedly do. Excellence then, is not an act but a habit."* –Aristotle
- *"The chains of habit are generally too small to be felt until they are too strong to be broken."* –Samuel Johnson.
- *"Most people don't have the willingness to break bad habits. They have a lot of excuses and they talk like victims."* –Carlos Santana
- *"Successful people are simply those with successful habits."* –Brian Tracy
- *"The only proper way to eliminate bad habits is to replace them with good ones."* –Jerome Hines
- *"Your net worth to the world is usually determined by what remains after your bad habits are subtracted from your good ones."* –Ben Franklin
- *"My bad habits aren't my title. My strengths and my talent are my title."* –Layne Staley

What are My Old Habits?

Scientists who study human behavior have found that more than 40 percent of the actions we perform each day aren't the result of conscious decisions but are the result of habits. A habit is a behavior, thought pattern, or emotional reaction that we have done or had so many times we engage in it without making a conscious choice to do so.

A habit is made up of three steps: Cue → Routine → Reward. When you go through the three steps of this loop, the habit comes to an end, until the next time there is a cue.

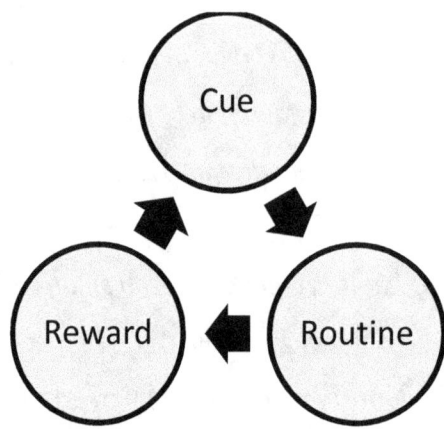

A cue is anything that triggers your brain to use one of the habits you have created. Cues can be just about anything: a smell, a picture, a sound, or even a thought.

A routine can be a set of behaviors, a thought pattern, or an emotional reaction. We often think of a habit as a behavior, but it doesn't have to be a behavior. We can also have emotional and cognitive habits.

The reward is the payoff that lets you know the habit is something you want to do again in the future. A reward can be just about anything, but it is usually something that makes us feel good, like chocolate, pride, or a compliment.

After you have created a habit, the habit is triggered by the cue, and your brain automatically and with little effort makes you go through the routine. The habit is completed when you get the reward. Unless you consciously work to stop or prevent a habit, most habits happen automatically.

If you are going to hold onto the positive changes you made by completing the assignments in this workbook, you are going to have to stop old habits from creeping into your life. The first step to stopping the return of old habits is to recognize when you are slipping back into those old habits. Then you must develop a plan for overcoming the bad habits.

Assignment

Identify five old habits you used during five different parts of your day before you started making the change to a citizen lifestyle. You are trying to identify bad habits that you used throughout the day when you were using behavior that hurt you and others, so it might help if you look for a bad habits from each of the following parts of your day: (1) waking up and getting ready to start your day, (2) leaving the house and going to school, (3) behavior while at school, (4) your routine after school, and (5) your bedtime routine. You might want to create a table like the one below when you complete this assignment.

	Cue	Routine	Reward
Wake-up			
Travel			
During day			
After school			
Bedtime			

Habit Control

You have to learn to control your old habits if you are going to live a citizen lifestyle. There is some good news and some bad news about habit control:

- **Good News** – Scientists have studied habit control, and we know for sure that you can change your habits. You can change old habits by creating new habits to replace the old habits. It sounds easier than it is, but the good news is that we know the secret of habit control: you can change a habit by replacing it with another habit.

- **Bad News** – You can never eliminate or erase an old habit. All you can do is put the old habit to sleep by using a replacement habit. If you always use the new habit, the old habit never awakens. If you do slip and the old habit does come back, keep in mind that the new habit you were using is only asleep. You can awaken the good habit by starting to use it again.

If you want to make an old habit go away, you have to create a new habit. You do this by changing the different parts of the habit loop.

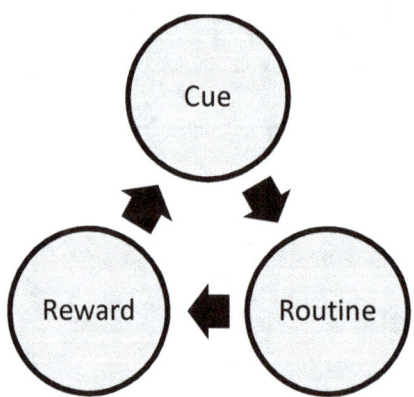

- **Cue** – You cannot eliminate cues. About the only thing you can do change the cue part of the habit loop is to reduce the number of times you come in contact with the cue for the old habit.

- **Routine** – This is the most important part of the habit loop when creating new habits. You have to create a new routine to use when the cue for the old habit pops up.
- **Reward** – Once you have created your new habit, you have to make sure it leads to a reward. The reward you get from the new routine may not be the exact reward you got from the old habit, but the new routine still has to be rewarding.

Changing a habit requires a lot of effort. You have to actually attack the old habit by creating a new habit that defeats the old habit. Once you create a new habit loop, it can become your habit. Your new habit will replace your old habit.

Assignment

Use the assignment that you completed in the previous lesson. List the cues from the previous assignment and then write a detailed plan for a new routine for each of the five cues. Once you have a new routine, you may notice that the rewards have changed. Be sure that you identify the reward you will get from the new routine.

	Cue	Routine	Reward
Wake-up			
Travel			
During day			
After school			
Bedtime			

Making Change Last

By now you know that if you want to change a habit you have to create a new habit to replace it. Creating a new habit is not difficult – what is difficult is making the new habit last. If you want to make a new habit last you have to believe you can change. Belief is the only thing that can make a new habit last.

From time to time, we all have really bad days. On those bad days, a new routine will not be enough to get you through. You need to believe in yourself and your new habit. You have to believe that you can cope by using the new habit and that you don't have to go back to using the old habit.

One of the most difficult things to do is to believe in isolation. Beliefs seem stronger and more real if the belief is shared with others. Belief is strongest when you are talking about your belief with others with similar beliefs.

If you want to make beliefs last, you have to talk with others about your new habit, and they have to support you. They have to believe what you believe. They have to believe that your new habit is the right thing to do and you can replace your old routine with a new routine.

| Create a new Routine | Find a support group | Believe in yourself |

You might doubt your ability to change, but if you are surrounded by people who believe in you, you might start to doubt your doubt. It is as if the change becomes real when we can see it other people's eyes. Once we believe that other people believe in us, we can believe in ourselves. Belief in ourselves is what makes change last.

Assignment

1. Make a list of ten reasons you believe that you can make the change and live a citizen lifestyle.

2. Make a list of people who can help you believe that you can make the change to a citizen lifestyle. Hint: The people in your support group could be helpful to you.

3. Share the list of reasons why you believe in yourself with the people you listed above. Ask them if they can give you one additional reason why you should believe in yourself.

My High-Risk Situations

A high-risk situation is any person, place, or thing that would make it easier for you to slip back into an old bad habit. A lot of people get fooled into thinking that a high-risk situation is just a place, but it is not. A high-risk situation can also be a person or thing.

- **High-Risk People** – A high-risk person is any person who would make it easy for your old habit to return. Someone you used to do drugs with or commit crimes with would be a high-risk person. Someone you victimized in the past would also be a high-risk person. People who don't believe in you are also high-risk.

- **High-Risk Places** – Some places make it easier for you to slip back into old habits. For example, if you had a problem with drugs and you were to go to a drug user's house, you would be in a high-risk place.

- **High-Risk Things** – Even objects can be a high-risk situation. For example, a bong would be a high-risk thing for a marijuana abuser. Throwing gang signs would be a high-risk thing for someone who used to be in a gang.

If you want to hold on to the positive changes you made as a result of completing assignments in this workbook, you need to be able to cope with your personal high-risk situations. In order to do that, you need to do three things. First, you need to be able to recognize your high-risk situations. Second, you need to have a plan for dealing with each of those high-risk situations. Third, you have to use the plan <u>every time</u> you come in contact with one of your high-risk situations.

Assignment

1. Make a list of your high-risk situations. At a minimum, you need to list three high-risk persons, three high-risk places, and three high-risk things. In other words, you should have at least nine high-risk situations listed.

2. For each of the high-risk situations on the list, write a coping plan. A coping plan is a positive, healthy way of avoiding, escaping, or eliminating the high-risk situation.

98

Coping with Relapse

Nobody is perfect. At any point, an old habit might pop up, and you could slip back into some old behavior. This is called a relapse. There are healthy and unhealthy ways of coping with relapse.

Healthy Ways to Cope with Relapse:

- **Risk of Relapse** – When the relapse happens, don't be mean to yourself. Admit to yourself that anyone, including you, can relapse.

- **Self-Awareness** – When a relapse happens, take a look at your habit loop. Try to identify the cues that triggered the old bad habit.

- **Skills** – When a relapse happens, spring into action and use your coping skills. You learned many coping skills during treatment, e.g., ACE and the Why Sandwich. Use your coping skills to deal with the relapse.

- **Support Group** – When a relapse happens, talk with your support group. Let them know you relapsed and let them know what you need from them, e.g., you need them to help you and believe in you.

Unhealthy Ways to Cope with Relapse:

- **Isolation** – If you cut ties with your support group after you relapse, you are just making things worse. Before you know it, you will be living a double life again.

- **Secrets** – If you start keeping secrets after your relapse, your secrets will make you sick, because secrets are poison. The more secrets you keep, the sicker you will become, and the further you will fall into your old bad habits.

- **Lower Standards** – One of the worst things you can do after a relapse is to lower your standards and tell yourself that you can't live a citizen lifestyle because it is too difficult. Once you lower your standards, you lose your belief in yourself.

- **Low Self-Esteem** – If you relapse and you become mean with yourself, you will tell yourself negative things, "Admit it. You can't change. Once a criminal, always a criminal." You will lose confidence in your ability to cope and to succeed.

Even if you do relapse, you can reverse a relapse. Relapses are no different than any other human behavior. You can always change.

The faster you respond to a relapse, the less likely it is that you will stay in a relapse. You can be sure that you will relapse if you do nothing. If you do relapse, do something and do it right away. Be quick with your coping – don't stay in relapse!

Do not blame yourself for relapses. This leads to a lower self-esteem. Instead of blaming yourself, perform a Why Sandwich and figure out how to cope with the situation.

When trying to overcome a relapse, don't focus on yourself. Try to figure out how to interrupt the relapse process when you see it happening. Successfully dealing with a relapse is not about YOU; it is about high-risk situations, cues to habits, and habit control.

Don't try to beat a relapse by yourself. Invite others to help you with the relapse. Rely upon your support group.

Relapse is a very slow process that happens over a long period of time. It is actually pretty hard to notice when you are relapsing. That is why you need to know the difference between effective and ineffective coping. Above all, when you notice that you are relapsing, do something healthy to get off that path.

Assignment

1. On one side of an index card, list ten signs that show that you are in a relapse.

2. On the other side of the index card, write ten things you can do to cope with a relapse. Hint: Some of the things you can do are listed in this lesson.

3. Carry this index card with you for one week. Look at the index card before breakfast, lunch, and dinner. If you notice any signs of relapse, flip the card over and use one of the coping techniques you listed.

Discharge Summary

When a treatment provider wraps up treatment with a client, the treatment provider writes a discharge summary, which serves to identify all the important changes that the client has made. It is only fitting that the last assignment in this workbook is a discharge summary that you write. You can use this discharge summary to remind yourself of the important changes you made. You can also use this discharge summary to keep you on the right track.

1. **Thinking** – Describe your style of thinking before you began this treatment program and now that you are preparing to move to aftercare. You can include such things as how you thought about yourself, your family, and society.

2. **Emotions** – Describe how your emotional functioning has changed as a result of being in this program. You can include such things as being able to label and express emotions.

3. **Relationships** – Describe your relationship style before treatment and now as you prepare to move to aftercare.

4. **Self-Management** – Do you have more control over yourself and your life? If so, explain. You might want to include how your self-control has changed with respect to your home life, work life, criminality, and sexuality.

5. **Personal Beliefs about Yourself** – Describe your self-concept before and after treatment. Your self-concept is all the beliefs that you have about yourself. How will you use your beliefs about yourself to make sure you live a citizen lifestyle?

Module Tests

If you benefit from this treatment program, what you learned during treatment sessions will make a difference outside of treatment sessions. The easiest way for you to be different outside treatment sessions is to take knowledge from the treatment sessions into your daily life. The easiest way you can do this is by memorizing what you have learned. If you want to make sure that you have memorized the new information, test yourself by taking and passing the module tests.

Traveler's Letter

1. What does it mean to say, "The traveler and the travel are not the same"?
2. What does it mean to say, "The person and the path are not the same"?
3. If you chose badly in the past, does that mean you are bad?
4. What can you do if you don't like the path you are on?
5. Can you stop change?
6. If change is going to happen anyway, do you think you should make choices and choose the change you want in your life?

Introduction

7. What is the fast-food approach to life?
8. What are the five reasons the fast-food approach to life will always fail?
9. What does it mean when we say the fast-food approach to life won't work because you are outnumbered?
10. How does being outnumbered lead to getting caught when you do bad things?
11. Why is the fast-food approach to life a really bad way to make money?
12. How come you can't keep the things you get by using the fast-food approach to life?
13. Why do you end up having less freedom when you use the fast-food approach to life?
14. What is the purpose of this workbook?
15. Explain "old me."
16. Explain "new me."
17. When are you supposed to complete assignments from this workbook?

18. Why is it okay to get feedback from the group on your assignments?

19. What are the three ways you can prove that you have changed?

20. What is an offense-specific workbook?

21. What is a psychoeducational workbook?

Module One: Orientation and Getting Ready to Change

22. Define "thinking error."

23. How can you use your knowledge of thinking errors to make sure you don't commit crimes?

24. Define "power play."

25. Define "closed channel."

26. Define "entitlement."

27. Define "victim stance."

28. Define "pet me."

29. Define "justifying."

30. Define "minimizing."

31. Define "super-optimism."

32. Define "ownership."

33. Define "making fools of others."

34. Define "can't wait."

35. Explain how to keep a thought journal.

36. What is the purpose of keeping a thought journal?

37. Define "criminal outlets."

38. Define "criminal precursor."

39. Name five criminal precursors.

40. How can you trick yourself into committing a crime by telling yourself there is a right way to do a wrong thing?

41. Define "criminal behavior."

42. What are the four ways you can show criminal behavior?

43. Define "citizen behavior."

44. What are the three criteria of citizen behavior?

45. Define "honesty."

46. In order to complete this program, what do you have to be honest about?

47. Name three good things that will happen if you are honest.

48. Name two reasons most people refuse to be honest about their problems.

49. Name the two ways you can make personal changes.

50. What are the four steps to change the easy way?

51. Define "self-awareness."

52. Define "self-monitoring."

53. Define "self-control."

54. Explain the hard way to change.

55. What are the steps of the hard way to change?

56. What is "limit testing"?

57. What is "the underground"?

58. What is the "the squeeze"?

59. What is "testing the waters?"

60. What does "conversion" mean?

61. Why should you change?

62. What causes lasting happiness?

63. Why is changing to a citizen lifestyle like detox?

64. Why does paranoia disappear after you switch to a citizen lifestyle?

65. Why do citizens have true power and criminals don't?

66. Do events cause emotions?

67. Explain how thoughts lead to emotions.

68. What are the two rules for solving problems?

69. What are the three parts of the Why Sandwich?

70. Explain each part of the why sandwich.

71. What does "ACE" stand for?

72. Explain how you can use avoidance to deal with problems.

73. Explain how you can use escape to deal with problems.

74. Explain how tunnel vision works.

75. Explain how thought broadcasting works.

76. Explain how a reality check works.

77. Explain how reversal works.

78. Explain how to use the golden rule to control your behavior.

79. What role does your supervising officer or staff members play as part of your treatment team?

80. What role does your treatment provider play as a member of your treatment team?

81. What role do members of your support group play as part of your treatment team?

82. What role do you play as a part of your treatment team?

Module Two: Honesty about Your Criminal Behavior

83. In order to be honest about your offense, what do you have to be honest about?

84. Why do you have to be honest about your criminal history?

85. Explain the saying, "Crime does not just happen."

86. Define "urge."

87. Define "fantasy."

88. Define "plan."

89. Define "set-up."

90. What are the four ways a criminal act might make a person feel good?

91. Is there such a thing as a victimless crime? Explain your answer.

92. Name at least two fantasies that criminals have about their victims.

93. How can a criminal use "first blood" as a way to justify committing a crime?

94. What does "double life" mean?

95. How does a criminal use a double life with his or her victim?

96. How does a criminal use a double life with family and friends?

97. What is the Offense Summary Worksheet?

98. What is your Fifth Amendment Right?

99. How do you protect your Fifth Amendment Right when completing the Criminal History Questionnaire?

Module Three: Self-Control

100. What does "modus operandi," or MO, mean?

101. What did the Cherokee wise man mean when he told his grandson that the wolf he feeds is the wolf who will live?

102. What are the "stair steps"?

103. Explain the role of thinking errors in the stair steps.

104. Explain the role of unpleasant emotions in the stair steps.

105. What kinds of plans can be part of the stair steps?

106. Define "trigger."

107. What is the healthy way of dealing with triggers?

108. What is the harmful way of dealing with triggers?

109. What is the Triple Column Technique?

110. What goes in the center column of the Triple Column Technique?

111. Why does the solution you write in the third column of the Triple Column Technique have to be believable?

112. What are the four basic emotions?

113. What is the root of anger?

114. What is the root of fear?

115. What is the root of sadness?

116. What is the harmful way of dealing with unpleasant emotions?

117. What is the healthy way of dealing with unpleasant emotions?

118. Explain the idea, "There is no right way to do a wrong thing."

119. What does "getting off the stair steps" mean?

Module Four: Your Support Group

120. What are some reasons that you might not want to tell your support group about the things that that your "old me" did?

121. Why is it a good thing to have your support group monitor you?

122. How can honesty help you form healthy relationships?

123. How can people in your support group help you during treatment?

124. How can people in your support group help you after treatment?

125. What is the purpose of your letter to your support group?

126. What is your contract with your support group?

127. Why is it important for you to let your support group know about the "new me"?"

128. Why is it important for you to ask your support group for praise and support?

129. What is splitting?

130. How does someone split his or her treatment provider and support group?

131. Once someone starts splitting, what is the quickest way to stop splitting?

132. How can resentment cause problems with your support group?

133. How can closed channel actions cause problems with your support group?

134. How can power play actions cause problems with your support group?

135. How can you use the Why Sandwich to help with your support group?

Module Five: Protecting Your Citizen Lifestyle

136. Explain why the experiment with the frogs and the hot water is important in understanding how we cope with stress.

137. How much of our daily behavior is due to habits?

138. What are the three steps of a habit loop?

139. What is the "cue" in the habit loop?

140. What is the "routine" in the habit loop?

141. What is the "reward" in the habit loop?

142. Can you change your habits?

143. What is the good news about habit change?

144. What is the bad news about habit change?

145. How do you change a bad habit?

146. What part of the habit loop do you focus on when creating a new habit?

147. Is it possible to change cues?

148. What are the two things you have to have to make a change in your habits last a long time?

149. Why is it important to get people to believe in you when you are trying to change your habits?

150. How can a support group help you make lasting changes in your habits?

151. Why is it important to believe in yourself if you want to make lasting habit changes?

152. What are "high-risk situations"?

153. What is a "high-risk person"?

154. What is a "high-risk place"?

155. What is a "high-risk thing"?

156. What is a "relapse"?

157. Does relapse come quickly or gradually? Explain your answer.

158. What are some healthy ways of coping with a relapse?

159. What are some unhealthy ways of coping with a relapse?

160. How fast should you respond to a relapse? Explain your answer.

161. Should you blame yourself for a relapse? Explain your answer.

162. How can low self-esteem make a relapse worse?

www.ingramcontent.com/pod-product-compliance
Lightning Source LLC
Chambersburg PA
CBHW081327310526
45789CB00018B/2456